De[illegible]

It was goo[illegible] to meet you & loved your energy.

Regards,

[illegible]
13/10/23

THE BRANDING BLUEPRINT

Become A Leader In Bathroom Fittings Industry

Amit Jain

Printed in India
First printing, 2023

Publisher name: Amit Jain

ISBN: 978-93-5917-105-0

Address: Flat NO. 002, tower-5, vipul greens, sector-48, sohna road, Gurgaon, Haryana - 122018

amazon : https://www.amazon.in/BRANDING-BLUEPRINT-Bathroom-Fittings-Industry/dp/9359171050

DEDICATION

This book is dedicated to all the passionate individuals and ambitious businesses in the bathroom fittings industry who strive for excellence and aim to make a lasting impact.

To the visionary leaders who dare to challenge the status quo, disrupt the industry, and push the boundaries of innovation. Your unwavering commitment to excellence inspires us all.

To the hardworking entrepreneurs who pour their heart and soul into building their brands, facing the ups and downs with unwavering determination. Your resilience and perseverance are truly admirable.

To the creative minds who bring forth fresh ideas, unique designs, and cutting-edge technologies that shape the future of the bathroom fittings industry. Your innovation and ingenuity drive the industry forward.

To the dedicated marketing professionals who tirelessly serve customers, going above and beyond to deliver exceptional experiences and build strong relationships. Your unwavering dedication to customer satisfaction is the backbone of our industry.

And finally, to the supportive families and loved ones who provide endless encouragement, understanding, and patience during the pursuit of our dreams. Your love and support make it all possible.

May this book serve as a valuable resource, guiding you towards success, growth, and the achievement of your goals in the bathroom fittings industry.

With heartfelt appreciation,
Amit Jain

ACKNOWLEDGEMENTS

I would like to express my deepest gratitude to everyone who has contributed to the creation and completion of this book. This would not have been possible without the support, encouragement, and expertise of numerous individuals and organizations.

I extend my heartfelt appreciation to my mentor and guide Akshar Yadav, whose valuable insights and guidance have helped me create this book. Your expertise and dedication to the subject matter have been instrumental in shaping my understanding of Branding, Marketing & Sales.

I would like to thank my father Mr. K. L. Jain for his love, support & belief in my abilities which has been a constant source of inspiration.

To my wife Divya Jain for always being the most amazing support in my life.

To all my customers and associates who have been a true inspiration in my professional journey.

To my colleagues and friends at 91 Springboard, who provided valuable feedback and constructive criticism during the writing process. Your insights and suggestions have played a significant role in refining and enhancing the content.

Once again, thank you to everyone who has been a part of this beautiful journey. Your contributions have made a lasting impact, and I am truly grateful for your support.

Warm regards,
Amit Jain

ABOUT THE AUTHOR

Amit Jain, born in 1976 in Gurgaon, is an accomplished professional who has made his mark in the family business which was started by his father Mr. K. L. Jain in 1972. After completing his graduation from Sri Venkateswara College, Delhi University in 1997, Amit decided to join the family business with a vision to take it to new heights. With his passion for the industry and a deep understanding of the market dynamics, he quickly became an integral part of Kesaria Rubber, a renowned company specialising in Rubber Sealing Solutions.

As an expert in the field of Rubber Parts, Amit Jain has played a pivotal role in the success and growth of Kesaria Rubber. With his keen eye for branding strategies, he has propelled the company to become a recognized name in the industry. Amit's commitment to quality and customer satisfaction has been instrumental in establishing Kesaria Rubber as a trusted source of high-quality rubber parts, across the globe.

Amit Jain is a devoted family man and is married to his loving wife, Divya. They have been together now for almost 23 years, supporting each other through life's ups and downs. Together, they have been blessed with two wonderful sons, Nuditt and Khoushil. Nuditt, their elder son, is 21 years old and is pursuing his college from University of Toronto, while

Khoushil, their younger son, is 15 years old and is a talented young individual.

Outside of his professional endeavours, Amit Jain has a zest for life and loves to explore the world. He is an avid traveller, always ready to embark on new adventures and discover different cultures. Exploring new destinations and immersing himself in diverse experiences broadens his perspective and fuels his creativity.

Beyond his passion for travel, Amit is known for his down-to-earth nature and approachability. He believes in the power of connections and values building meaningful relationships with people from all walks of life. Amit's friendly demeanour and open-mindedness make him a pleasure to work with and an inspiring leader.

With his vast knowledge of the Rubber Industry, Amit Jain continues to shape the growth and success of Kesaria Rubber. Through his leadership, branding acumen, and commitment to quality, he is poised to lead the company to even greater heights, solidifying its position as a leader in the field of PTFE & Rubber Sealing Solutions.

PREFACE

Welcome to **"The Branding Blueprint: Become A Leader in Bathroom Fittings Industry."** This book is the culmination of years of experience, insights, and lessons learned by Mr. Amit, a seasoned professional in the bathroom fittings industry. With a deep passion for branding and a relentless pursuit of excellence, Amit has dedicated himself to helping individuals and businesses establish themselves as leaders in this competitive market.

In today's fast-paced business landscape, branding plays a crucial role in shaping the success of any industry. It is no different for the bathroom fittings industry, where standing out and capturing the attention of the target audience is essential. In this book, Amit shares his wealth of knowledge and practical strategies that can empower aspiring leaders to position their brands effectively and carve a niche for themselves.

This book is designed as a comprehensive guide that covers every aspect of branding, from understanding the market landscape to creating a compelling brand identity, and from implementing effective marketing strategies to building strong customer relationships. With each chapter, Amit provides valuable insights, real-life examples, and actionable steps that readers can apply to their own branding journeys.

Drawing on his own experiences and successes, Amit shares the challenges he faced, the lessons he learned, and the strategies he implemented to build a reputable brand in the bathroom fittings industry. Through his book, he aims to inspire and guide readers towards their own path to success.

Whether you are a budding entrepreneur, a marketing professional, or an industry enthusiast, **"The Branding Blueprint: Become A Leader in Bathroom Fittings Industry"** offers valuable insights and practical advice that can transform your brand's presence and elevate it to new heights. It is a roadmap that empowers readers to navigate the intricacies of branding and make informed decisions that align with their vision and goals.

I encourage you to dive into the pages of this book, absorb the knowledge shared by Amit, and apply it to your own journey in the bathroom fittings industry. Embrace the power of branding, harness the strategies outlined within, and unlock your potential to become a leader in this dynamic market.

Remember, building a strong brand is not just about products and services; it is about creating a lasting impression, establishing trust, and delivering exceptional value. Let this book be your guide to unlocking the full potential of your brand and achieving remarkable success.

Wishing you an enlightening and transformative reading experience.

CONTENT

CHAPTER 01

THE BATHROOM FITTINGS INDUSTRY LANDSCAPE

An overview of the industry, its history, key players, and current trends

Introduction to the Bathroom Fittings Industry

The bathroom fittings industry is a significant sector in the global economy. It encompasses the production, distribution, and sale of a wide range of products, including faucets, showers, bathtubs, toilets, and other related accessories. These items are essential in residential, commercial, and public buildings, making the industry a crucial part of modern infrastructure. The quality and functionality of bathroom fittings greatly impact the overall user experience, making them an integral part of any construction or renovation project.

Moreover, the industry holds significant economic importance. The demand for bathroom fittings remains consistently high due to population growth, urbanization, and increasing standards of living across the globe. This sustained demand creates business opportunities for manufacturers, suppliers, retailers, and service providers within the industry, stimulating economic growth and job creation.

The bathroom fittings industry is constantly evolving to meet the changing needs and preferences of consumers. Several notable trends and innovations have emerged in recent years, shaping the industry's landscape and driving its growth, such as:

1. **Sustainability:** With growing environmental consciousness, sustainability has become a significant focus in the industry. Manufacturers are incorporating eco-friendly materials, water-saving technologies, and energy-efficient features into their products to reduce environmental impact.

2. **Smart Technology:** The integration of smart technology into bathroom fittings has revolutionized the way we interact with these products. Smart showers, touchless faucets, and voice-activated toilets are just a few examples of how technology has enhanced convenience, efficiency, and hygiene in the bathroom.

3. **Design Aesthetics:** The aesthetics of bathroom fittings have become increasingly important to consumers. Modern designs, sleek finishes, and customizable options allow individuals to create personalized and visually appealing spaces.

4. **Wellness and Comfort:** The industry is witnessing a growing focus on wellness and comfort, with features such as therapeutic showers, heated toilet seats, and water massage systems gaining popularity. These innovations aim to enhance relaxation and promote well-being in the bathroom environment.

History of the Bathroom Fittings Industry

From the invention of the flush toilet in the 19th century to the introduction of innovative features such as touchless faucets and smart toilets in recent years, the industry has continuously adapted to meet the evolving needs and expectations of consumers. From the rudimentary plumbing systems of ancient civilizations to the luxurious and technologically advanced fittings of today, the industry has seen a remarkable transformation. Key milestones include the advent of indoor plumbing, the mass production of porcelain fixtures, and the incorporation of digital technology into bathroom design. Throughout history, advancements in materials, manufacturing techniques, and design have revolutionized the industry.

The history of the bathroom fittings industry in India is an interesting narrative that reflects the country's cultural, social, and technological advancements over the centuries. Let's explore the journey of the bathroom fittings industry in India:

Early Sanitation Practices: India has a rich history of sanitation practices dating back thousands of years. Ancient civilizations in the Indus Valley, such as Mohenjo-Daro and Harappa, had advanced systems of sanitation, including underground drainage systems and well-planned bathrooms with water channels. These early practices highlight the importance given to hygiene and sanitation even in ancient times.

Influence of Colonial Era: The arrival of the British during the colonial era brought significant changes to India's sanitation practices and infrastructure. The British introduced modern plumbing systems, including water supply networks and sewage systems, in major cities like Kolkata, Mumbai, and Chennai. This marked a turning point in the development of bathroom fittings in India.

Traditional Bathroom Fixtures: Prior to the advent of modern bathroom fittings, traditional fixtures were prevalent in Indian households. These included squat toilets, known as "Indian-style" toilets, which are still widely used in rural areas. Other traditional fixtures included metal or earthenware pitchers and basins for water storage and handwashing. These fixtures were often simple in design and functioned based on gravity flow principles.

Emergence of Indian Manufacturers: With India's independence in 1947, the country witnessed the emergence of indigenous manufacturers in the bathroom fittings industry. Indian companies began producing a range of bathroom fixtures, including faucets, showers, sanitaryware, and accessories. These manufacturers aimed to cater to the growing domestic demand for modern and aesthetically pleasing bathroom fittings.

Technological Advancements: In the late 20th century, technological advancements played a crucial role in shaping the bathroom fittings industry in India. The introduction of new materials, such as ceramic and stainless steel, improved the durability and aesthetic appeal of bathroom fixtures. Innovations in manufacturing techniques and processes led to increased production efficiency and product quality.

Market Liberalization and Globalization: The liberalization of the Indian economy in the 1990s and the subsequent wave of globalization brought significant changes to the bathroom fittings industry. International brands entered the Indian market, offering a wide range of innovative products and design choices. This led to increased competition and raised the bar for quality and design standards in the industry.

Design Evolution and Aesthetic Preferences: As India underwent rapid urbanization and socio-cultural changes, design preferences in bathroom fittings evolved as well. The demand for aesthetically pleasing and functionally advanced products grew. Indian consumers started embracing contemporary and minimalist designs, as well as luxury and designer collections. The industry responded to these changing preferences by offering a diverse range of products to cater to various tastes and budgets.

Focus on Sustainability and Water Conservation: In recent years, there has been a growing emphasis on sustainability and water conservation in the bathroom fittings industry in India. With water scarcity being a significant challenge in many parts of the country, manufacturers have introduced water-saving technologies such as low-flow faucets and dual-flush toilets. These eco-friendly practices have gained traction among consumers who prioritize environmental responsibility.

Digital Transformation and E-commerce: The digital revolution and the widespread adoption of e-commerce platforms have significantly impacted the bathroom fittings industry in India. Consumers now have access to a wide range of products online, allowing them to compare prices, read reviews, and make informed purchasing decisions. E-commerce platforms have also facilitated the entry of smaller and niche bathroom fittings brands, expanding consumer choices in the market.

Government Initiatives and Regulations: The Indian government has introduced various initiatives and regulations to promote sanitation and improve the quality of bathroom fittings. The Swachh Bharat Abhiyan (Clean India Mission) launched in 2014 aims to ensure access to clean and functional toilets for all citizens. Additionally, there are regulations in place to ensure the quality and safety standards of bathroom fittings, including certification requirements and testing procedures.

Future Outlook: The bathroom fittings industry in India is poised for further growth and innovation. With rapid urbanization, rising disposable incomes, and a focus on modern lifestyles, the demand for high-quality and technologically advanced bathroom fittings is expected to increase. The industry is likely to witness continued investments in research and development, leading to the introduction of innovative products that cater to the evolving needs and preferences of Indian consumers.

The history of the bathroom fittings industry in India showcases the country's journey towards modernization and its commitment to improving sanitation practices. From ancient civilizations to the present day, the industry has undergone significant transformations, offering a wide range of innovative and aesthetically pleasing products to meet the diverse needs of Indian consumers.

Key Players in the Industry

The bathroom fittings industry is populated by a diverse range of manufacturers, brands, and retailers that compete to offer innovative products and exceptional customer experiences. Several brands and companies have played pivotal roles in shaping the bathroom fittings industry.

In India, the bathroom fittings industry has witnessed significant growth and development, driven by the country's rapid urbanization, rising disposable income, and increasing demand for modern and aesthetically pleasing bathrooms.

Several key players have emerged as leaders in the Indian bathroom fittings market, contributing to its evolution and competitiveness. Let's explore some of the prominent key players in the bathroom fittings industry in India, who have made significant contributions through their innovative designs, quality products, and commitment to sustainability:

1. **Jaquar** is India's leading bathroom fittings brands, known for its wide range of products, innovative designs, and superior quality. With a strong presence both in India and abroad, Jaquar offers a comprehensive portfolio of faucets, showers, sanitaryware, wellness products, and accessories. The brand is synonymous with reliability, durability, and customer satisfaction.

2. **Kohler** entered the Indian market in 2006 and quickly gained prominence due to its high-quality products and innovative designs. The brand offers a comprehensive range of bathroom fittings, including faucets, showers, sanitaryware, bathtubs, and accessories. Kohler's products are widely available across India through a network of authorized dealers, showrooms, and retail outlets.

3. **Hindware,** a brand under the flagship of HSIL Limited, is another major player in the Indian bathroom fittings industry. Hindware offers a diverse range of products, including faucets, sanitaryware, showers, bathtubs, and allied bathroom accessories. The brand is recognized for its contemporary designs, superior craftsmanship, and commitment to customer service.

4. **CERA** is a leading player in the Indian bathroom fittings market, offering a wide range of products that combine innovation, functionality, and style. CERA's product portfolio

includes faucets, sanitaryware, tiles, mirrors, and wellness products. The brand is known for its emphasis on quality, durability, and affordability.

5. **Parryware**, a division of Roca Bathroom Products Pvt. Ltd., is a well-established brand in the Indian bathroom fittings industry. With a legacy of over 60 years, Parryware offers a comprehensive range of sanitaryware, faucets, showers, and bathroom accessories. The brand is known for its elegant designs, advanced technology, and commitment to sustainable practices.

In addition to these established players, the Indian market also welcomes new entrants and niche players who bring unique offerings, specialized products, and targeted solutions for specific customer segments. The competitive landscape of the Indian bathroom fittings industry continues to evolve, driven by consumer demands, technological advancements, and market dynamics. These key players, along with several other regional and international brands, have shaped the Indian bathroom fittings industry through their product offerings, brand reputation, and commitment to customer satisfaction. They have introduced innovative designs, advanced technologies, and sustainable practices, catering to the diverse needs and preferences of Indian consumers.

As the Indian economy grows and the real estate and construction sectors flourish, the demand for quality bathroom fittings is expected to further escalate. Key players in the industry will continue to play a crucial role in meeting this demand, driving innovation, and shaping the future of the bathroom fittings market in India.

Current Market Size and Economic Impact

The bathroom fittings industry is a multi-billion-dollar sector. It contributes significantly to economies worldwide, providing employment opportunities and aiding in the development of manufacturing and retail sectors. The industry's growth is influenced by factors such as real estate development, population growth, and consumer spending habits.

The bathroom fittings industry in India has experienced significant growth over the years, driven by factors such as urbanization, rising disposable incomes, changing lifestyles, and increasing awareness about sanitation and hygiene. Let's explore the current market size and economic impact of the bathroom fittings industry in India:

Market Size and Growth: The bathroom fittings industry in India has witnessed steady growth, fuelled by the demand for modern and aesthetically pleasing bathroom fixtures. According to industry reports, the market size of the bathroom fittings industry in India was valued at around USD 2.5 billion in 2020. The market is expected to continue its growth trajectory, with a projected CAGR of around 10% from 2021 to 2026.

Residential Sector: The residential sector is a key driver of the bathroom fittings industry in India. As more people move to urban areas and upgrade their living spaces, there is a growing demand for well-designed and functional bathroom fixtures. The increasing trend of apartment complexes and high-rise buildings further contributes to the demand for bathroom fittings.

Commercial and Hospitality Sectors: The commercial and hospitality sectors also play a significant role in the bathroom fittings industry. The rapid growth of commercial spaces, such as office complexes, retail outlets, and shopping malls, drives the demand for high-quality and durable bathroom fixtures. Additionally, the booming hospitality industry, including hotels, resorts, and restaurants, requires premium bathroom fittings to provide a comfortable and luxurious experience for guests.

Rise of Real Estate and Infrastructure Development: India's robust real estate and infrastructure development activities have a direct impact on the bathroom fittings industry. The construction of residential and commercial properties, along with infrastructure projects such as airports, hospitals, educational institutions, and government buildings, generates demand for bathroom fixtures and accessories. The government's initiatives such as the Smart Cities Mission and Housing for All further drive the growth of the industry.

Increasing Awareness about Sanitation and Hygiene: With the increasing emphasis on sanitation and hygiene, there is a growing awareness among consumers about the importance of well-equipped bathrooms. The government's Swachh Bharat Abhiyan (Clean India Mission) has played a pivotal role in promoting sanitation practices and creating a demand for quality bathroom fittings. This awareness has led to a shift in consumer preferences towards modern, water-efficient, and hygienic bathroom fixtures.

Technological Advancements and Product Innovation: Technological advancements have revolutionized the bathroom fittings industry in India. Manufacturers are incorporating smart technologies, touchless sensors, and water-saving mechanisms into their products, catering to the evolving needs of consumers. The industry is witnessing innovations in areas such as digital faucets, thermostatic shower systems, and smart toilets, offering convenience, water conservation, and enhanced user experiences.

Employment and Skill Development: The bathroom fittings industry in India contributes significantly to employment generation and skill development. The industry encompasses various segments, including manufacturing, distribution, retail, and after-sales service, creating employment opportunities at different levels. The industry's growth also fosters skill development initiatives, as professionals require technical expertise in areas such as plumbing, installation, and maintenance of bathroom fittings.

Contribution to the Economy: The bathroom fittings industry plays a crucial role in the Indian economy. It contributes to the country's GDP through manufacturing activities, job creation, tax revenues, and exports. The growth of the industry has also encouraged investments in research and development, infrastructure development, and technological advancements, which further boost economic growth.

In short, the bathroom fittings industry in India is witnessing robust growth, driven by factors such as urbanization, rising disposable incomes, infrastructure development, and increasing awareness about sanitation and hygiene. The industry's market size is expanding, with a positive outlook for the future. It not only contributes to the economy but also plays a vital role in enhancing the quality of life for Indian consumers by providing innovative, functional, and aesthetically pleasing bathroom fixtures.

Industry Trends

The bathroom fittings industry is experiencing several notable trends on a global scale. These trends reflect the changing preferences and demands of consumers, as well as the advancements in technology and sustainability practices. One significant trend is the focus on sustainability and water conservation. With growing environmental concerns, manufacturers are developing water-efficient products, such as low-flow faucets and dual-flush toilets, to minimize water consumption. Another trend is the integration of smart technology into bathroom fittings. Smart faucets, showers, and toilets with touchless sensors, temperature control, and voice-activated features are gaining popularity for their convenience and enhanced user experience. Design aesthetics also play a crucial role, with a shift towards minimalistic and contemporary styles, as well as the use of premium materials like stainless steel and natural stone. Additionally, there is a rising demand for accessible and inclusive bathroom fittings to cater to the needs of people with disabilities or limited mobility. These industry trends indicate a dynamic and innovative landscape that is constantly evolving to meet the evolving needs and expectations of consumers worldwide.

The bathroom fittings industry in India is also witnessing several noteworthy trends that reflect the evolving preferences and demands of Indian consumers. One significant trend is the growing focus on hygiene and sanitation, driven by initiatives like the Swachh Bharat Abhiyan (Clean India Mission). Consumers are increasingly seeking bathroom fittings that are easy to clean, have antimicrobial properties, and promote overall cleanliness. Another trend is the emphasis on water-saving solutions. With water scarcity being a critical issue in many parts of the country, manufacturers are developing water-efficient faucets, showers, and toilets that help conserve water without compromising performance. Design aesthetics also play a vital role, with Indian consumers showing a preference for contemporary and minimalist designs, as well as unique and culturally inspired motifs. Additionally, there is a rising demand for smart bathroom fittings that offer convenience and automation, such as touchless sensors and smart toilets with advanced features. These trends indicate a shift towards sustainable, hygienic, and technologically advanced bathroom fittings that cater to the specific needs and aspirations of Indian consumers.

Consumer Behaviour and Preferences

Consumer behaviour and preferences play a crucial role in shaping the bathroom fittings industry. Understanding the factors that influence consumer choices helps manufacturers and retailers tailor their products and marketing strategies to meet the needs and expectations of their target audience. The choice of materials plays a significant role in determining the quality, durability, aesthetics, and overall satisfaction of consumers. Here are some key aspects of consumer behaviour and preferences in the bathroom fittings industry:

Design and Aesthetics: Consumers place great importance on the design and aesthetics of bathroom fittings. They seek products that enhance the overall visual appeal of their bathrooms and complement the overall interior design of their homes. Contemporary and minimalist designs are particularly popular, as they offer a clean and sophisticated look. The materials used in bathroom fittings greatly influence their aesthetics and design. Consumers are drawn to fittings that exhibit a visually appealing appearance and harmonize with the overall style of their bathrooms. Materials like chrome, brushed nickel, and porcelain provide a polished and sophisticated look, while natural materials like stone or wood can add a touch of warmth and organic beauty.

Quality and Durability: Consumers value the quality and durability of bathroom fittings. They prefer products that are made from high-quality materials and offer long-lasting performance. Stainless steel, brass, and ceramic are commonly preferred materials due to their durability and resistance to corrosion. Also, bathroom fittings, when designed and manufactured with high-quality rubber materials, contribute to the overall durability of the fittings. They provide resistance against wear, corrosion, and degradation over time, ensuring that the fittings maintain their functionality and performance for an extended period.

Functionality and Ease of Use: Consumers look for bathroom fittings that are functional and easy to use. Features such as smooth operation, ergonomic designs, and intuitive controls are highly desirable. Water-saving mechanisms, like low-flow faucets and dual-flush toilets, are also favoured by environmentally conscious consumers. Rubber parts, such as gaskets and seals, help facilitate smooth movement and operation of handles, valves, and other components. They reduce friction and provide a comfortable user experience, allowing consumers to effortlessly control the water flow and temperature.

Hygiene and Cleanliness: In recent years, there has been an increased emphasis on hygiene and cleanliness in bathroom fittings. Consumers seek products that are easy to clean and maintain, with antimicrobial surfaces and self-cleaning features. The use of antimicrobial coatings on surfaces is also gaining popularity for its ability to inhibit the growth of bacteria and maintain a clean environment. This is particularly relevant in the current context of heightened awareness regarding hygiene practices. Consumers are increasingly concerned about hygiene and cleanliness in bathroom fittings, and the choice of materials plays a significant role in addressing these concerns. Non-porous materials like porcelain and stainless steel are highly preferred as they are easier to clean, resistant to stains, and less likely to harbour bacteria or germs.

Water Efficiency: With water scarcity being a concern in many regions, consumers prioritize water-efficient bathroom fittings. They look for products that minimize water wastage without compromising performance. Water-saving technologies, such as aerators and flow restrictors, are seen as favourable options. Rubber parts, internal fittings, flow restrictors and aerators, help regulate and control the flow of water, ensuring that it is used efficiently without compromising performance. These parts contribute to water-saving efforts, aligning with the sustainability preferences of consumers.

Smart and Connected Solutions: The rise of smart technology has influenced consumer preferences in the bathroom fittings industry. Consumers are increasingly interested in smart fittings that offer advanced features such as touchless operation, temperature control, and personalized settings. Connected solutions that integrate with home automation systems are also gaining popularity.

Price and Value for Money: Price and value for money are crucial considerations for consumers in the bathroom fitting industry. While consumers seek products that offer durability, functionality, and aesthetic appeal, they also want them to be affordable and provide long-term value. Price plays a significant role in consumer decision-making, as it directly impacts their purchasing power and budget constraints. Consumers compare prices across different brands and products, evaluating the features and benefits they offer in relation to the cost. Value for money is determined by the overall quality, performance, and durability of the bathroom fittings in relation to their price. Consumers are willing to invest in bathroom fittings that offer a balance between quality and affordability, seeking products that provide long-term benefits and meet their expectations. They consider factors such as the reputation of the brand, warranty or after-sales service, and the durability of materials used. Bathroom fittings that offer a competitive price point while delivering reliable performance, innovative features, and a pleasing aesthetic are highly sought after by consumers. It is essential for manufacturers and retailers to provide transparent pricing, clearly communicate the value proposition of their products, and demonstrate how their offerings provide a favourable balance between price and quality. By offering affordable and value-driven options, the bathroom fitting industry can cater to a wide range of consumer budgets and ensure customer satisfaction.

Sustainability and Environmental Impact: The bathroom fittings industry in India is increasingly focusing on sustainability and reducing its environmental impact. With growing awareness of environmental issues and the need for responsible consumption, both manufacturers and consumers are prioritizing sustainable practices in the industry. Manufacturers are adopting eco-friendly manufacturing processes, utilizing recycled materials, and implementing energy-efficient production methods. They are also developing water-saving technologies, such as low-flow faucets, water-efficient showers, and dual-flush toilets, to minimize water consumption. Furthermore, the industry is placing emphasis on waste management and recycling to reduce the environmental footprint of bathroom fittings. Consumers are actively seeking sustainable bathroom fittings that align with their environmental values. The integration of renewable energy sources in manufacturing facilities and the use of eco-friendly packaging materials are additional steps taken towards sustainability. By embracing sustainable practices and offering eco-friendly options, the bathroom fittings industry in India is contributing to a greener future and meeting the evolving demands of environmentally conscious consumers.

In Conclusion, the introduction to the bathroom fittings industry provides a comprehensive overview of its significance in the modern world. The industry encompasses a wide range of products, including faucets, showers, bathtubs, toilets, and accessories, which are essential components of residential, commercial, and public buildings. The chapter highlights the historical development of the industry, tracing its evolution from basic plumbing fixtures to innovative and technologically advanced solutions. It emphasizes the importance of key players in shaping the industry and highlights the current market size and economic impact. Furthermore, the chapter discusses the emerging trends in the industry, such as the focus on sustainability, smart technology, and design aesthetics. Understanding consumer behaviour and preferences is crucial for manufacturers and retailers to cater to the diverse needs and expectations of consumers. The chapter concludes by emphasizing the significance of rubber parts, such as O-rings, in ensuring the proper functioning and longevity of bathroom fittings. Overall, the introduction provides a solid foundation for understanding the bathroom fittings industry and sets the stage for exploring the various aspects in greater detail in the subsequent chapters.

CHAPTER 02

UNDERSTANDING BRANDING

A deep dive into what branding is, its importance, and how it can differentiate a business in the market

Branding plays a pivotal role in the success of any business, and the bathroom fittings industry is no exception. In this chapter, we look into the concept of branding and its significance in establishing a strong presence and reputation in the market. We explore how effective branding strategies can differentiate bathroom fittings companies, build customer loyalty, and drive business growth. By understanding the principles and practices of branding, industry players can position themselves as leaders and gain a competitive edge.

The Essence of Branding

Defining Branding: Branding encompasses much more than a company's logo or visual identity. It represents the intangible aspects of a brand, such as its reputation, values, and emotional connection with consumers. At its core, branding is about shaping the perception of a brand in the minds of consumers and creating a distinct identity that sets it apart from competitors. It involves carefully crafting the brand's messaging, visual elements, and overall brand experience to resonate with the target audience. By defining branding in this comprehensive manner, bathroom fittings companies can better understand its role in building trust, establishing a unique market position, and fostering long-term customer loyalty. With a clear understanding of branding, companies can embark on developing effective strategies to shape and manage their brand's identity in a competitive industry landscape.

Importance of Branding in the Bathroom Fittings Industry: Effective branding is essential for companies operating in this competitive market as it serves multiple purposes. Firstly, branding helps establish trust and credibility among consumers. When customers are faced with numerous options, a strong and well-recognized brand instills confidence and assurance in their purchase decisions. Secondly, branding enables companies to convey their unique value proposition. By defining what sets them apart from competitors, companies can showcase their expertise, quality craftsmanship, innovative designs, and commitment to customer satisfaction. Thirdly, branding creates a distinct identity that resonates with consumers. Through consistent messaging, visual elements, and brand experiences, companies can build a strong brand image that connects emotionally with their target audience. This emotional connection fosters customer loyalty, encourages repeat business, and facilitates word-of-mouth recommendations. By understanding the importance of branding, bathroom fittings companies can invest in strategic brand-building efforts to differentiate themselves and thrive in a competitive market.

Building a Strong Brand Identity

Identifying Brand Purpose and Values: A brand's purpose goes beyond the mere selling of products; it encapsulates the reason why the brand exists and the positive impact it aims to make in the lives of its customers. By clearly defining and communicating its purpose, a bathroom fittings brand can connect with consumers on a deeper level, aligning with their values and aspirations.

Additionally, identifying the core values that guide the brand's behaviour and decision-making is crucial. These values serve as guiding principles that shape the brand's culture, relationships with stakeholders, and overall brand experience. For example, a brand may prioritize sustainability, craftsmanship, innovation, or customer-centricity as its core values.

By defining a brand's purpose and values, bathroom fittings companies can create a strong foundation for their brand identity. This clarity not only helps in internal alignment but also resonates with consumers who share similar values. When a brand's purpose and values are authentically communicated, it builds trust, enhances brand loyalty, and fosters long-term relationships with customers.

Furthermore, a clear brand purpose and values act as a compass for decision-making and strategy development. They provide a framework for product development, marketing campaigns, and customer engagement initiatives. By staying true to their purpose and values, bathroom fittings companies can differentiate themselves from competitors, attract like-minded customers, and create a lasting impact in the industry.

In conclusion, identifying a brand's purpose and values is a foundational step in brand development for bathroom fittings companies. It allows them to connect with customers on an emotional level, build trust, and guide decision-making. By embracing a purpose-driven approach and aligning with core values, these companies can create a strong brand identity that resonates with consumers and sets them apart in the competitive market.

Developing a Memorable Brand Name and Logo:

In this section, we explore the process of developing a memorable brand name and logo for bathroom fittings companies. A brand name and logo are the visual representations of a brand's identity and play a crucial role in capturing the attention of consumers and creating a lasting impression.

The brand name serves as the foundation of the brand's identity. It should be carefully chosen to reflect the brand's personality, values, and target audience. A well-crafted brand name is memorable, unique, and easy to pronounce. It should evoke positive associations and convey the essence of the brand's offerings. For bathroom fittings companies, the brand name could incorporate elements that highlight quality, innovation, or a specific design aesthetic, thereby positioning the brand in the minds of consumers.

In addition to the brand name, a well-designed logo is essential for creating visual recognition and brand recall. The logo should visually represent the brand's identity, values, and key attributes. It should be visually appealing, simple, and versatile, allowing for easy application across various marketing materials and platforms. For bathroom fittings companies, the logo design could incorporate elements that symbolize water, sleekness, or a unique design feature associated with their products. Colours, typography, and graphic elements should be carefully chosen to evoke the desired emotions and align with the overall brand image.

When developing a brand name and logo, it is essential to conduct thorough research to ensure they are not already in use by competitors or have negative connotations. Trademark availability and legal considerations should be taken into account to avoid potential conflicts and protect the brand's intellectual property rights.

By investing time and effort into developing a memorable brand name and logo, bathroom fittings companies can establish a distinct visual identity that resonates with consumers. A well-crafted brand name and logo increase brand recognition, create a sense of professionalism, and contribute to building trust and credibility. They serve as a visual representation of the brand's values, quality, and commitment to excellence.

In conclusion, developing a memorable brand name and logo is a critical aspect of brand development for bathroom fittings companies. A carefully chosen brand name and a well-designed logo help differentiate the brand, create visual recognition, and convey the desired brand image. With a strong brand name and logo, bathroom fittings companies can make a lasting impression on consumers, stand out in a competitive market, and establish a foundation for building a successful brand identity.

Crafting a Compelling Brand Story: In this section, we explore the importance of crafting a compelling brand story and messaging for bathroom fittings companies. A brand story goes beyond the features and benefits of the products; it communicates the brand's values, purpose, and the unique journey that led to its formation. It engages consumers on an emotional level, connecting them with the brand's identity and creating a sense of authenticity and relatability.

Crafting a brand story involves understanding the brand's history, values, and the aspirations it fulfils for its customers. It highlights the brand's passion, expertise, and commitment to delivering exceptional bathroom fittings. The story should be well-crafted, engaging, and align with the target audience's desires and aspirations.

Furthermore, developing consistent brand messaging is crucial for effectively communicating the brand's value proposition and differentiating it from competitors. The messaging should be clear, concise, and impactful, conveying the brand's key attributes, benefits, and positioning in the market. It should resonate with the target audience and address their pain points, demonstrating how the brand's products and solutions can meet their needs and enhance their bathroom experiences.

To craft a compelling brand story and messaging, bathroom fittings companies should consider conducting market research to gain insights into customer preferences, desires, and pain points. This research will help shape the brand narrative, ensuring it resonates with the target audience and effectively communicates the brand's unique selling proposition.

Consistency in brand messaging is essential across all touchpoints, including marketing materials, advertising campaigns, social media content, and customer interactions. This consistency reinforces the brand's identity and helps build recognition and familiarity among consumers. It also contributes to establishing trust and credibility, as customers perceive consistent messaging as a sign of professionalism and reliability.

By crafting a compelling brand story and messaging, bathroom fittings companies can differentiate themselves in the market, forge an emotional connection with consumers, and foster brand loyalty. A well-crafted brand story and consistent messaging build brand equity, enhance brand recognition, and position the brand as a trusted and preferred choice among consumers.

In conclusion, crafting a compelling brand story and messaging is a crucial aspect of branding for bathroom fittings companies. It allows them to effectively communicate their values, purpose, and unique selling proposition to consumers. By engaging consumers on an emotional level and delivering consistent messaging, these companies can differentiate themselves, build brand loyalty, and establish a strong brand presence in the market.

Example of a Brand Story for a Bathroom Fittings Company:

Meet AquaD - The Story of Elegance and Functionality

"At AquaD, our brand story is inspired by the pursuit of elegance and functionality in every bathroom experience. It all began with a vision to transform ordinary bathrooms into extraordinary sanctuaries, where people could indulge in relaxation and luxury.

Our founder, Ankit Sabharwal, had a deep passion for design and a desire to create bathroom fittings that blended timeless aesthetics with innovative functionality. Drawing inspiration from nature's elements and architectural wonders, he embarked on a journey to redefine the bathroom fittings industry.

Ankit believed that a well-designed bathroom should be a haven of serenity, a place where one could escape the stresses of everyday life. With this vision in mind, he assembled a team of talented designers, engineers, and artisans who shared her passion for excellence.

Together, they embarked on a quest to create bathroom fittings that seamlessly integrated style, durability, and performance. Hours of meticulous craftsmanship, extensive research, and continuous innovation resulted in a range of products that exceeded expectations.

But AquaD's story goes beyond exceptional products. It's a story of a brand that deeply cares about the environment and sustainability. We believe that beautiful design and responsible practices can coexist. Our commitment to eco-friendly manufacturing processes, water conservation, and use of sustainable materials is at the core of everything we do.

Our brand story is about transforming bathrooms into personal sanctuaries that reflect individual style and elevate the everyday experience. From sleek faucets that perfectly blend form and function to luxurious shower systems that envelop you in a cascade of rejuvenating water, every AquaD product is meticulously designed to inspire and delight.

But our story doesn't end with our products. It extends to the relationships we build with our customers. We strive to create a seamless and enjoyable experience from the moment you explore our website to the installation of our fittings in your home. Our dedicated customer service team is always ready to assist, ensuring your satisfaction and peace of mind.

At AquaD, we believe that everyone deserves a bathroom that reflects their unique style and enhances their well-being. Our brand story is a testament to our unwavering commitment to excellence, quality, and customer satisfaction.

Join us on this journey of elegance and functionality. Experience the AquaD difference and transform your bathroom into a sanctuary of beauty and tranquility."

Learning From This Story

It's multifaceted and can have several positive effects on AquaD as a brand:

1. **Emotional Connection:** The brand story creates an emotional connection with customers by sharing the founder's passion and vision. It evokes a sense of inspiration and aspiration, allowing customers to relate to the brand on a deeper level. This emotional connection fosters brand loyalty and a long-lasting relationship with customers.

2. **Differentiation:** The brand story sets AquaD apart from competitors by highlighting its unique approach to blending elegance and functionality. It showcases the brand's commitment to craftsmanship, innovation, and sustainability, positioning AquaD as a distinctive and desirable choice in the market.

3. **Brand Image and Reputation:** The story reinforces AquaD's brand image as a trusted and reputable company that values quality, design, and customer satisfaction. It enhances the brand's reputation as a leader in the bathroom fittings industry, known for its exceptional products and dedication to eco-friendly practices.

4. **Customer Engagement:** The brand story invites customers to be part of the AquaD journey, creating a sense of community and engagement. It encourages customers to

explore the brand further, interact with its products, and share their experiences, fostering a strong brand-customer relationship.

5. **Market Positioning:** The impact of this story helps AquaD establish a strong market position as a premium brand that offers both style and functionality. It positions AquaD as a brand that understands the needs and desires of customers, providing them with a transformative bathroom experience.

6. **Competitive Advantage:** The unique brand story of AquaD serves as a competitive advantage, allowing the brand to stand out in a crowded market. It gives customers a compelling reason to choose AquaD over other options, as they connect with the brand's values, sustainability efforts, and commitment to excellence.

Brand Communication and Positioning

In the competitive landscape of the bathroom fittings industry, effective brand communication and positioning are crucial for companies to establish a strong presence, differentiate themselves, and connect with their target audience. This section explores the significance of brand communication and positioning strategies and their impact on brand perception and customer engagement.

Brand Identity and Messaging: Brand identity encompasses the visual and verbal elements that define a company's personality, values, and unique offerings. In the bathroom fittings industry, creating a compelling brand identity is essential for standing out amidst numerous competitors. This includes designing a visually appealing logo, selecting appropriate brand colours, and developing a consistent tone of voice for all communication.

Crafting a strong brand message is equally important. Companies must clearly articulate their value proposition, highlighting what sets them apart from competitors. This includes emphasizing product features, quality, design aesthetics, and any unique selling points that resonate with the target market. A well-crafted brand message helps create a memorable impression and builds recognition and trust among customers.

Target Audience Segmentation: Understanding the target audience is vital for effective brand communication. The bathroom fittings industry caters to diverse consumer segments, including residential homeowners, commercial builders, interior designers, and architects. By segmenting the target audience based on demographics, preferences, and purchase behaviour, companies can tailor their communication strategies to resonate with specific customer groups.

Segmentation allows companies to develop targeted messaging, create relevant content, and choose appropriate communication channels. For example, marketing efforts targeting residential homeowners may focus on aesthetics, ease of installation, and maintenance, while communication aimed at commercial builders might emphasize durability, cost-effectiveness, and compliance with industry regulations.

Multi-channel Communication: With the proliferation of digital platforms, effective brand communication in the bathroom fittings industry requires a multi-channel approach. Companies must strategically leverage various channels such as websites, social media, email marketing, industry publications, and trade shows to reach and engage with their target audience.

A well-designed and user-friendly website serves as a central hub for brand information, showcasing products, and providing resources for customers. Social media platforms offer opportunities to share engaging content, customer testimonials, and design inspirations. Email marketing allows companies to directly communicate with existing customers and nurture leads.

Industry publications and trade shows provide avenues for companies to showcase their expertise, demonstrate product innovations, and connect with industry professionals. By utilizing a mix of online and offline channels, companies can create a comprehensive brand presence and reinforce their brand message consistently across platforms.

Brand Positioning: Brand positioning refers to how a company differentiates itself in the minds of customers. In the bathroom fittings industry, companies can position themselves based on various factors, such as product quality, design innovation, sustainability, or price. The chosen positioning should align with the target audience's needs and preferences and highlight the unique value proposition of the brand.

Effective brand positioning requires a deep understanding of the competitive landscape. Companies should conduct thorough market research to identify gaps, analyse competitors' positioning strategies, and identify opportunities to occupy a distinctive space in the market. By positioning themselves strategically, companies can attract their ideal customers, build brand loyalty, and gain a competitive advantage.

In conclusion, brand communication and positioning are critical elements in the success of companies operating in the bathroom fittings industry. By developing a strong brand identity, tailoring messages to target audiences, utilizing multi-channel communication, and strategically positioning their brand, companies can effectively engage customers, differentiate themselves from competitors, and build a favourable brand image. A cohesive and compelling brand communication strategy not only attracts customers but also strengthens brand loyalty, fosters long-term relationships, and drives business growth.

Brand Experience and Customer Engagement

In the bathroom fittings industry, creating a positive brand experience and engaging customers is essential for building long-term relationships, fostering brand loyalty, and driving business growth. This section explores the importance of brand experience and customer engagement strategies and their impact on customer satisfaction and advocacy.

Brand Experience: Brand experience encompasses every touchpoint a customer has with a company, from initial awareness to post-purchase interactions. It involves creating a seamless and memorable journey that aligns with the brand's values, promises, and customer expectations.

A consistent and cohesive brand experience begins with the first interaction a customer has with the brand, whether it's through a website, showroom, or advertising. It continues throughout the customer's purchase journey, including product selection, purchasing process, installation, and after-sales support.

Companies in the bathroom fittings industry can enhance brand experience by focusing on several key factors. These include product quality and reliability, providing helpful and knowledgeable customer support, ensuring efficient product delivery and installation services, and offering warranties and post-sales assistance. By delivering a positive brand experience at every touchpoint, companies can leave a lasting impression on customers and differentiate themselves from competitors.

Customer Engagement: Customer engagement refers to the interactions and activities that foster a deeper connection between a company and its customers. Engaged customers are more likely to become brand advocates, provide feedback, and remain loyal to the brand over time.

By prioritizing customer engagement, companies can build a loyal customer base, generate positive word-of-mouth referrals, and gain valuable insights to improve their products and services. In the bathroom fittings industry, there are various strategies to enhance customer engagement. These include:

1. **Personalized Communication:** Companies can leverage customer data and preferences to deliver personalized communication through email marketing, targeted offers, and tailored content. By addressing customers' specific needs and interests, companies can create a more meaningful connection.

2. **Customer Feedback and Surveys:** Encouraging customers to provide feedback and opinions about their experience with the brand and products can help companies understand their needs and improve their offerings. Surveys, reviews, and testimonials can be used to gather insights and make data-driven decisions.

3. **Social Media Engagement:** Active presence on social media platforms allows companies to engage with customers, respond to queries, share design inspirations, and encourage user-generated content. Social media platforms can also serve as a space for customers to connect with each other and share their experiences.

4. **Loyalty Programs:** Implementing loyalty programs and rewards for repeat customers can incentivize continued engagement and foster brand loyalty. Offering exclusive discounts, VIP access, or special events can make customers feel valued and appreciated.

5. **Community Building:** Creating online communities or forums where customers can interact with each other, share experiences, and seek advice can foster a sense of belonging and strengthen the relationship between the brand and its customers.

In conclusion, brand experience and customer engagement are critical aspects of success in the bathroom fittings industry. By delivering a consistent and positive brand experience at every touchpoint, companies can differentiate themselves and leave a lasting impression on customers. Through personalized communication, gathering feedback, utilizing social media, implementing loyalty programs, and fostering a sense of community, companies can engage customers, build relationships, and foster brand loyalty. By focusing on creating exceptional brand experiences and engaging customers, companies can drive customer satisfaction, advocacy, and long-term business success.

Brand Extension and Innovation

In the ever-evolving bathroom fittings industry, brand extension and innovation play a vital role in maintaining a competitive edge and expanding market reach. This section explores the significance of brand extension and innovation strategies and their impact on brand growth and customer perception.

Brand Extension: Brand extension refers to leveraging the existing brand equity and reputation to introduce new products or enter new market segments. It allows companies to capitalize on their established brand identity, customer loyalty, and market presence to explore new business opportunities.

In the bathroom fittings industry, brand extension can take various forms. It can involve introducing new product lines, such as expanding from faucets and showers to include bathroom accessories like towel racks, soap dispensers, or mirrors. It can also involve entering related market segments, such as kitchen fittings or plumbing fixtures.

Brand extension provides several benefits. Firstly, it allows companies to cater to the evolving needs and preferences of their existing customer base, providing them with a comprehensive range of products under a trusted brand. Secondly, it enables companies to tap into new customer segments and expand their market share. Lastly, brand extension enhances brand visibility and reinforces the brand's image as an industry leader and innovator.

However, successful brand extension requires careful consideration and planning. Companies must ensure that the extension aligns with their core brand values, maintains product quality and consistency, and resonates with the target audience. It is crucial to conduct market research, analyse customer needs and preferences, and develop a comprehensive marketing strategy to support the brand extension.

Innovation: Innovation is a driving force in the bathroom fittings industry, enabling companies to stay relevant, differentiate themselves, and meet changing customer demands. It involves the development and introduction of new technologies, designs, and functionalities to enhance the overall user experience.

Innovation in the bathroom fittings industry can encompass various aspects, including product design, materials, water-saving technologies, smart functionalities, and sustainability initiatives. Companies are continuously investing in research and development to create products that offer improved performance, energy efficiency, durability, and ease of use.

By embracing innovation, companies can gain a competitive advantage. Innovative products can attract attention, generate excitement, and position the brand as a leader in the industry. Additionally, innovation allows companies to address emerging trends and consumer preferences, such as eco-friendly solutions, touchless technology, or customizable designs.

To foster innovation, companies in the bathroom fittings industry often collaborate with designers, architects, and technology experts. They also actively seek feedback from customers, conduct market research, and monitor industry trends to identify areas for improvement and identify opportunities for innovation.

Successful implementation of brand extension and innovation strategies requires a balance between maintaining the brand's core values and embracing new possibilities. By strategically extending the brand and embracing innovation, companies can expand their market presence, attract new customers, and reinforce their position as industry leaders.

In conclusion, brand extension and innovation are essential strategies for sustained growth and competitiveness in the bathroom fittings industry. Brand extension allows companies to leverage their existing brand equity and enter new market segments, while innovation enables them to meet evolving customer demands and differentiate themselves. By carefully planning and executing brand extension initiatives and fostering a culture of innovation, companies can drive brand growth, capture new market opportunities, and solidify their position in the industry.

One notable example of innovation in the bathroom fittings industry in India is the introduction of water-saving technologies and eco-friendly solutions. With increasing awareness about water conservation and environmental sustainability, many companies have developed innovative products that help reduce water consumption without compromising on performance and user experience.

For instance, some bathroom fittings manufacturers have introduced **dual-flush toilets** that offer two flushing options: a full flush for solid waste and a half flush for liquid waste. This feature allows users to control the amount of water used per flush, resulting in significant water savings over time. These toilets often incorporate advanced flushing mechanisms and optimized bowl designs to ensure efficient flushing even with reduced water volume.

In addition to water-saving toilets, there have been innovations in faucets and showers as well. **Companies have developed aerators and flow restrictors** that mix air with water, creating a steady flow while reducing water consumption. These innovative fittings maintain a comfortable water pressure while minimizing wastage, making them more sustainable and cost-effective for consumers.

Furthermore, the integration of smart technology into bathroom fittings has been another area of innovation. Companies have introduced **smart showers and faucets that allow users to control water temperature, flow, and duration** through smartphone apps or voice commands. These smart fittings not only enhance convenience but also enable users to monitor and manage water usage, promoting water conservation.

Another aspect of innovation in the bathroom fittings industry is the use of eco-friendly materials and manufacturing processes. Companies are increasingly adopting sustainable practices, such as using recycled materials, reducing energy consumption during production, and implementing eco-friendly packaging solutions. These initiatives aim to minimize the environmental impact of the industry and provide customers with more sustainable choices.

Overall, the bathroom fittings industry in India has witnessed significant innovation in water-saving technologies, smart functionalities, and sustainable practices. These innovations not only address the evolving needs of consumers but also contribute to water conservation and environmental sustainability. By embracing innovation, companies in the industry are driving positive change and shaping a more sustainable future for the bathroom fittings sector in India.

In conclusion, understanding branding is vital for the success of bathroom fittings companies. By establishing a strong brand identity, communicating effectively, delivering exceptional experiences, and embracing innovation, companies can build enduring relationships with consumers and differentiate themselves in the market. A well-crafted brand strategy and implementation can lead to increased brand recognition, customer loyalty, and ultimately, business growth. This chapter sets the foundation for exploring branding principles further and provides insights into how bathroom fittings companies can establish themselves as industry leaders through effective branding strategies.

CHAPTER 03

THE POWER OF A STRONG BRAND

Exploring successful case studies of powerful brands in the bathroom fittings industry and what we can learn from them

In the highly competitive bathroom fittings industry, building and maintaining a strong brand is crucial for success. A strong brand goes beyond a company's logo or product offerings. It encompasses the overall perception, reputation, and emotional connection that customers have with the brand. This chapter describes the power of a strong brand in the bathroom fittings industry and explores how it influences customer loyalty, market positioning, and business growth.

Brand Recognition and Trust

Brand recognition and trust play a pivotal role in the success of a brand in the bathroom fittings industry. When customers encounter a familiar brand, it instills a sense of confidence and trust in the quality and reliability of the products. This recognition and trust are built over time through consistent brand messaging, visual identity, and positive customer experiences.

Brand recognition refers to the ability of customers to identify and recall a brand based on its logo, name, or other visual cues. In the bathroom fittings industry, where numerous brands compete for customers' attention, having strong brand recognition is essential for standing out in the marketplace. A recognizable brand is more likely to be top-of-mind when customers are considering bathroom fittings for their homes or businesses.

Trust is another critical factor that influences customer purchasing decisions. Customers are more likely to choose a brand they trust, as it provides them with confidence in the product's quality, performance, and longevity. Building trust requires consistently delivering on promises, meeting customer expectations, and providing excellent customer service. Brands that prioritize customer satisfaction and maintain high standards of quality and craftsmanship earn the trust of their customers.

One of the key drivers of brand recognition and trust is effective marketing and communication strategies. Brands invest in various marketing channels to create awareness and establish a positive perception in the minds of consumers. This includes traditional advertising, digital marketing campaigns, social media engagement, public relations efforts, and participation in industry events and trade shows. Consistent messaging across these channels helps reinforce the brand's presence and builds trust among consumers.

Another aspect that contributes to brand recognition and trust is the brand's reputation and track record. Positive reviews, testimonials, and word-of-mouth recommendations from satisfied customers can significantly enhance a brand's reputation and instil trust in potential buyers. Brands that prioritize quality, customer satisfaction, and ethical business practices tend to build a positive reputation, which further strengthens their brand recognition and trustworthiness.

To enhance brand recognition and trust, brands in the bathroom fittings industry should focus on delivering consistent and exceptional experiences throughout the customer journey. This includes providing clear product information, transparent pricing, responsive customer support, and reliable warranties or guarantees. Brands that prioritize communication and transparency foster stronger relationships with customers, which, in turn, leads to increased brand recognition, trust, and loyalty.

In conclusion, brand recognition and trust are vital elements in the bathroom fittings industry. A strong brand that is recognized and trusted by customers has a significant competitive advantage. It not only attracts new customers but also retains existing ones and fosters brand loyalty. By consistently delivering on promises, providing exceptional customer experiences, and maintaining a positive reputation, brands can strengthen their brand recognition and trust, ultimately driving business growth and success.

Differentiation and Competitive Advantage

In the highly competitive bathroom fittings industry, differentiation is key to standing out from the competition and gaining a competitive advantage. A strong brand understands the importance of creating a unique identity that sets it apart from other players in the market.

Differentiation starts with defining a brand's unique selling propositions (USPs) and identifying what sets it apart from competitors. In the bathroom fittings industry, this could include factors such as innovative designs, superior craftsmanship, advanced technologies, or a focus on sustainable practices. By highlighting these distinctive attributes, a brand can position itself as a leader and attract customers who resonate with its values, design aesthetics, and overall brand experience.

One aspect of differentiation in the bathroom fittings industry is innovative product designs. Brands that invest in research and development to create unique and eye-catching designs gain a competitive edge. These designs may focus on functionality, aesthetics, or a combination of both. By offering products with innovative features and designs, a brand can capture the attention of customers who seek bathroom fittings that not only serve a practical purpose but also enhance the overall look and feel of their spaces.

Superior craftsmanship is another factor that sets brands apart in the bathroom fittings industry. Attention to detail, precision engineering, and high-quality materials contribute to the overall durability and performance of the products. Brands that prioritize superior craftsmanship communicate their commitment to excellence and quality, which resonates with discerning customers who value long-lasting and reliable bathroom fittings.

Advanced technologies also play a role in differentiation within the bathroom fittings industry. Brands that leverage technology to offer smart and connected bathroom fittings, such as digitally controlled showers or sensor-activated faucets, provide added convenience and functionality to customers. These innovative technologies not only enhance the user experience but also position the brand as forward-thinking and at the forefront of industry trends.

Sustainable practices and environmentally friendly initiatives are increasingly becoming important differentiators in the bathroom fittings industry. Brands that prioritize sustainable materials, water conservation, and eco-friendly manufacturing processes align themselves with the growing consumer demand for environmentally conscious products. By adopting sustainable practices, brands can attract customers who value sustainability and contribute to a greener future.

To effectively differentiate a brand, it is essential to communicate the unique selling propositions clearly and consistently through various marketing channels. This includes showcasing the brand's distinctive features and benefits in advertising campaigns, social media content, product packaging, and website messaging. By effectively communicating the brand's differentiation, it becomes easier to capture the attention of customers and position the brand as a leader in the bathroom fittings industry.

In conclusion, differentiation is crucial for brands in the bathroom fittings industry to gain a competitive advantage. By identifying and highlighting their unique selling propositions, brands can create a distinct identity that resonates with customers. Whether through innovative designs, superior craftsmanship, advanced technologies, or sustainable practices, differentiation sets a brand apart, attracts customers, and contributes to long-term success in the market.

Customer Loyalty and Advocacy

Customer loyalty and advocacy are crucial for the success and growth of any brand in the bathroom fittings industry. When customers develop a strong sense of loyalty towards a brand, they become repeat purchasers, brand ambassadors, and advocates who actively promote and recommend the brand to others.

Loyalty is built through consistently delivering exceptional customer experiences at every touchpoint. Bathroom fittings brands that prioritize customer satisfaction, product reliability, and responsive customer support are more likely to foster strong customer loyalty. By exceeding customer expectations and providing personalized interactions, brands can create a positive emotional connection with their customers, leading to long-term loyalty.

Building customer loyalty goes beyond the initial purchase. Brands should strive to maintain ongoing engagement and communication with their customers. This can be achieved through loyalty programs, exclusive offers, personalized recommendations, and proactive customer support. By nurturing the relationship with customers, bathroom fittings brands can create a sense of belonging and make customers feel valued and appreciated.

Customer loyalty also translates into advocacy, where loyal customers actively promote and endorse the brand to their networks. Advocacy can take various forms, including positive word-of-mouth recommendations, online reviews, and social media engagement. When customers are satisfied with their bathroom fittings products and experiences, they are more likely to share their positive opinions with others, generating valuable organic marketing for the brand.

To encourage customer advocacy, brands can provide opportunities for customers to share their experiences, such as through social media campaigns, testimonials, or referral programs. By leveraging the power of customer testimonials and user-generated content, bathroom fittings brands can amplify their reach and credibility, attracting new customers and reinforcing the brand's reputation.

Customer loyalty and advocacy contribute to the overall success of a bathroom fittings brand by driving customer retention, increasing brand awareness, and influencing purchase decisions. Loyal customers not only continue to choose the brand for their own needs but also become influential brand ambassadors who expand the brand's reach and influence.

By prioritizing customer satisfaction, building strong relationships, and creating exceptional experiences, bathroom fittings brands can foster customer loyalty and advocacy. These loyal and passionate customers become invaluable assets for the brand, contributing to its growth, reputation, and long-term sustainability in the industry.

Premium Pricing and Profitability

A strong brand in the bathroom fittings industry often commands premium pricing. Customers are willing to pay more for products associated with a reputable brand that offers superior quality, design, and reliability. Premium pricing contributes to higher profit margins and profitability for the brand.

However, premium pricing is not solely based on the brand's reputation. It must be supported by delivering exceptional value to customers through product performance, durability, and aesthetics. Brands must consistently meet or exceed customer expectations to justify the premium pricing and maintain their market position.

Investing in strategic marketing and branding efforts is essential for establishing a premium image and attracting customers willing to pay higher prices. This includes crafting compelling brand stories, creating visually appealing marketing materials, and utilizing premium channels and platforms to reach the target audience. Consistent brand messaging and a cohesive brand identity can reinforce the perception of premium value.

Also, providing an exceptional customer experience can justify premium pricing. This includes offering personalized consultations, expert advice, and seamless after-sales service. By going above and beyond customer expectations and creating a positive emotional connection, brands can build customer loyalty and justify higher prices.

Overall, achieving premium pricing and profitability in the bathroom fittings industry requires a combination of factors, including differentiation, brand reputation, product quality, design, effective marketing, and customer experience. By consistently delivering value, creating a strong brand image, and targeting the right customer segment, brands can position themselves as premium providers and maximize profitability.

Brand Expansion and Diversification

A strong brand opens doors for expansion and diversification within the bathroom fittings industry. Successful brands have the opportunity to extend their product lines, introduce new collections, or venture into related market segments. Customers who have established trust and loyalty with a brand are more likely to explore and embrace new offerings under the same brand umbrella. It refers to strategic initiatives taken by a company to extend its brand presence into new markets, product categories, or customer segments. It involves leveraging the existing brand equity, customer base, and expertise to create profitable business opportunities beyond the company's current offerings.

Brand expansion typically involves introducing new products or services that complement or enhance the existing offerings. This allows the company to meet the evolving needs and preferences of its customers while capitalizing on its established brand reputation. By expanding the product portfolio, companies can cater to a broader range of customer segments and increase their market share.

Diversification, on the other hand, involves entering completely new markets or industries that may be unrelated to the company's existing business. This strategy aims to reduce reliance on a single market or product category and create new avenues for growth. Diversification can be either related, where there are some synergies or similarities between the new and existing businesses, or unrelated, where the new business is entirely distinct from the existing operations.

Brand expansion and diversification offer several benefits to a company:

1. **Market Reach:** By expanding into new markets or introducing new products, a company can reach a wider customer base and tap into previously untapped opportunities. This can lead to increased sales and revenue streams.

2. **Reduced Risk:** Diversifying the business helps mitigate risks associated with fluctuations in specific markets or

industries. It spreads the company's exposure and reduces dependency on a single market, making the business more resilient to economic downturns or industry-specific challenges.

3. **Enhanced Brand Value:** Successful brand expansion and diversification efforts can enhance the overall brand value and reputation. It demonstrates the company's ability to innovate, adapt, and cater to changing customer needs, positioning it as a dynamic and forward-thinking brand.

4. **Cross-Selling and Upselling Opportunities:** Brand expansion allows companies to cross-sell and upsell their products or services to existing customers. By offering a broader range of offerings, companies can increase customer loyalty and maximize customer lifetime value.

5. **Competitive Advantage:** A well-executed brand expansion or diversification strategy can provide a competitive edge in the market. It allows companies to differentiate themselves from competitors by offering a unique combination of products or services and capturing market segments that others may not be targeting.

However, brand expansion and diversification also come with certain challenges and risks. It requires thorough market research, understanding of customer needs, and careful evaluation of market dynamics. Companies must ensure that the new offerings align with the brand's values, maintain consistent quality standards, and deliver a positive customer experience.

Overall, brand expansion and diversification are strategic initiatives that enable companies to explore new growth opportunities, increase market share, and create sustainable business models. By leveraging their existing brand equity, companies can extend their reach and drive long-term success in a competitive marketplace.

Story of the Leader in Bathroom Fittings Industry in India-JAQUAR

In the bustling city of Delhi, originated a bathroom fittings company named Jaquar. Started as a modest family-owned business, Mr. N. L. Mehra had a vision to revolutionize the bathroom industry and JAQUAR became a household name known for its exceptional quality and innovative designs.

Jaquar began by manufacturing and selling high-quality faucets and bathroom accessories in 1960. Their commitment to excellence and customer satisfaction earned them a loyal customer base and a reputation for reliability. Building upon this success, Jaquar embarked on a journey of brand expansion and diversification.

Recognizing the growing demand for complete bathroom solutions, Jaquar expanded its product portfolio to include sanitaryware, bath tubs, and wellness products. This strategic move allowed them to offer customers a comprehensive range of bathroom solutions, ensuring that every aspect of the bathroom experience could be fulfilled by Jaquar.

To support their brand expansion, Jaquar invested in state-of-the-art manufacturing facilities and cutting-edge technology. They focused on research and development, collaborating with international designers and engineers to create innovative and aesthetically pleasing products that combined functionality with style. This commitment to design excellence positioned Jaquar as a trendsetter in the industry.

In addition to expanding their product range, Jaquar established exclusive showrooms that showcased not only their bathroom fittings but also curated bathroom designs that reflected the latest trends and provided customers with inspiration for their own spaces. This holistic approach to the bathroom experience differentiated Jaquar from its competitors and attracted a discerning clientele.

As Jaquar's brand continued to grow, they identified new opportunities for diversification. They ventured into the lighting industry, introducing a range of innovative and energy-efficient LED lighting solutions for both residential and commercial spaces. Leveraging their expertise in design and engineering, Jaquar created lighting products that seamlessly integrated with their bathroom fittings, providing a cohesive and aesthetically pleasing experience for customers.

Furthermore, Jaquar recognized the potential in the hospitality sector. They collaborated with luxury hotels and resorts, offering customized bathroom solutions that met the unique requirements of these establishments. By catering to the specific needs of the hospitality industry, Jaquar established itself as a trusted partner for top-tier hotels, elevating their brand image and generating substantial business opportunities.

Through their strategic brand expansion and diversification efforts, Jaquar transformed from a bathroom fittings manufacturer into a comprehensive bathroom solutions provider. Their commitment to quality, innovation, and customer satisfaction enabled them to create profitable business ventures in various sectors.

Today, Jaquar is not only a leading brand in the bathroom fittings industry but also a symbol of excellence and luxury. Their brand expansion and diversification strategies have allowed them to capitalize on new markets and revenue streams while staying true to their core values. Jaquar's success story stands as a testament to the power of vision, innovation, and adaptability in creating a profitable and sustainable business in the competitive bathroom industry.

So, in a nutshell, *a strong brand in the bathroom fittings industry commands a competitive advantage, drives customer loyalty, and fosters long-term success. By focusing on brand recognition, trust, differentiation, communication, customer engagement, and innovation, brands can build a powerful presence in the market and establish themselves as leaders in the industry. The power of a strong brand not only influences customer purchasing decisions but also shapes the overall perception and success of a brand in the bathroom fittings industry.*

CHAPTER 04

IDENTIFYING YOUR UNIQUE SELLING PROPOSITION (USP)

A guide to identifying and articulating what makes your brand unique in the bathroom fittings industry

Identifying Your Unique Selling Proposition (USP) is a crucial step in building a successful brand in the bathroom fittings industry. Your USP is what sets you apart from your competitors and communicates the unique value that your brand offers to customers. It is the key message that differentiates your brand and influences customers' purchasing decisions. Here is a guide to help you identify and articulate your USP:

Analyse Your Competitors

Analysing your competitors in the bathroom fittings industry is a critical step in identifying your Unique Selling Proposition (USP) and positioning your brand effectively. Start by conducting a comprehensive analysis of your competitors in the bathroom fittings industry. Understand their product offerings, pricing strategies, target market, and brand positioning. Identify the gaps or areas where your brand can stand out. Here are some key considerations when conducting competitor analysis:

Product Offerings: Evaluate the range of products offered by your competitors. Look at the different types of bathroom fittings they provide, including faucets, showers, bathtubs, toilets, and accessories. Assess the variety, quality, and features of their products to understand how they meet customer needs.

Pricing Strategies: Examine the pricing strategies employed by your competitors. Determine whether they position themselves as premium, mid-range, or budget brands. Analyse how their pricing aligns with the perceived value they offer. Identify any pricing gaps in the market that your brand can fill.

Target Market: Identify the target market segments your competitors focus on. Determine if they cater to specific customer demographics, such as residential, commercial, or luxury segments. Understand their positioning and messaging to these target markets.

Brand Positioning: Assess how your competitors position their brands in the market. Consider factors such as their brand messaging, values, and positioning statements. Look for unique selling points they emphasize and how they differentiate themselves from other brands.

Marketing and Promotion: Analyse the marketing and promotional strategies used by your competitors. Examine their advertising campaigns, website content, social media presence, and any special promotions or events. Determine the channels they use to reach their target audience and the messaging they convey.

Customer Reviews and Feedback: Read customer reviews and feedback about your competitors' products and services. Identify common pain points, complaints, or areas in which customers express dissatisfaction. This will help you understand the gaps or opportunities where your brand can excel.

Distribution Channels: Evaluate the distribution channels utilized by your competitors. Determine if they primarily sell through retail stores, online platforms, or a combination of both. Assess their distribution network's reach and effectiveness in serving the target market.

Industry Trends and Innovations: Stay updated on the latest industry trends and innovations within the bathroom fittings industry. Identify any emerging technologies, materials, or design concepts that your competitors are leveraging. This will help you identify areas for differentiation or potential gaps in the market.

By conducting a thorough analysis of your competitors, you gain valuable insights into the existing landscape of the bathroom fittings industry. This analysis will help you identify areas where your brand can stand out, offer unique value, and create a strong USP. It allows you to understand the competitive landscape, differentiate your brand effectively, and position yourself strategically in the market. Remember, competitor analysis is an ongoing process as the market evolves, and new players enter the industry. Continuously monitor and adapt your strategies to maintain a competitive edge.

Understand Your Target Market

Gain a deep understanding of your target market's needs, preferences, and pain points. Conduct market research, surveys, and customer interviews to gather valuable insights. Identify the specific problems or challenges your target customers face in relation to bathroom fittings. Here are some key aspects to consider when understanding your target market:

Demographics: Start by defining the demographic characteristics of your target customers. This includes factors such as age, gender, income level, education, and occupation. Understanding these demographics helps you tailor your products, messaging, and marketing strategies to resonate with your intended audience.

Psychographics: Dive deeper into the psychographic profile of your target market. This involves understanding their lifestyle, values, interests, and preferences. Explore their attitudes towards bathroom fittings, their aspirations, and how they perceive the importance of aesthetics, functionality, and sustainability.

Needs and Pain Points: Identify the specific needs, challenges, and pain points that your target customers face when it comes to bathroom fittings. Are they seeking durability, water efficiency, ease of installation, or innovative features? Understanding their pain points helps you position your brand as the solution to their problems.

Purchase Behaviour: Analyse the purchase behaviour of your target market. Determine how they research, evaluate, and make buying decisions for bathroom fittings. Are they influenced by price, quality, design, brand reputation, or recommendations from others? This information helps you align your marketing strategies to meet their expectations.

Competitor Interaction: Study how your target market engages with your competitors. Identify the brands they currently prefer and why. Explore the gaps or areas where your competitors may fall short in meeting their needs. This knowledge allows you to position your brand as a superior alternative.

Emerging Trends: Stay updated on emerging trends and shifts in consumer behaviour within the bathroom fittings industry. Monitor changes in design preferences, sustainability concerns, technological advancements, and any other factors that impact your target market. Adjust your strategies to align with these evolving trends.

Market Research: Conduct surveys, focus groups, and interviews with your target customers to gather insights directly from them. Ask questions about their preferences, pain points, and what they value most in bathroom fittings. This primary research provides valuable data to shape your USP.

Feedback and Reviews: Analyse customer feedback, reviews, and ratings of your own brand and your competitors. Pay attention to the positive aspects which customers appreciate and the areas where improvements are needed. This feedback helps you refine your USP to better align with customer expectations.

By understanding your target market deeply, you can develop a strong USP that resonates with their needs and preferences. This knowledge enables you to tailor your product offerings, marketing messages, and customer experiences to create a compelling value proposition. It also helps you identify opportunities for innovation and differentiation that can set your brand apart from competitors. Keep a pulse on your target market's evolving needs and adapt your strategies accordingly to maintain a competitive edge.

Assess Your Unique Strengths

To identify your Unique Selling Proposition (USP) in the bathroom fittings industry, it is essential to assess your unique strengths. Evaluate your brand's unique strengths, capabilities, and resources. Consider factors such as product quality, design innovation, manufacturing processes, customer service, sustainability initiatives, or technological advancements. This involves understanding what sets your brand apart from competitors and leveraging those strengths to create a competitive advantage. Here are some key aspects to consider when assessing your unique strengths:

Product Differentiation: Evaluate the unique features and benefits of your bathroom fittings products. What makes them stand out in terms of design, functionality, durability, or innovation? Assess how your products address specific customer needs or solve common pain points in a distinctive way.

Quality and Reliability: Assess the quality standards of your bathroom fittings. Do you adhere to rigorous quality control processes to ensure superior craftsmanship and long-lasting performance? Highlight any certifications, warranties, or industry accolades that demonstrate your commitment to delivering high-quality products.

Design and Aesthetics: Examine the design aesthetics of your bathroom fittings. Do you offer stylish and visually appealing options that cater to different customer preferences? Consider whether your designs reflect the latest trends or showcase unique and timeless elements that differentiate your brand.

Material Selection: Evaluate the materials used in your bathroom fittings. Are they of premium quality, environmentally friendly, or technologically advanced? Highlight any sustainable or innovative materials that contribute to the overall value and appeal of your products.

Manufacturing Expertise: Assess your manufacturing capabilities and expertise. Do you have advanced production facilities, skilled craftsmen, or proprietary manufacturing processes that give you a competitive edge? Highlight any unique aspects of your manufacturing that contribute to the superior quality and performance of your products.

Brand Reputation and Trust: Consider the reputation and trust associated with your brand. Have you built a strong reputation for delivering exceptional products and customer service? Highlight any customer testimonials, industry awards, or positive reviews that reinforce your brand's credibility and reliability.

Customer Service and Support: Evaluate the level of customer service and support you provide. Do you offer personalized assistance, prompt responses to inquiries, and efficient after-sales support? Highlight any initiatives or programs that demonstrate your commitment to ensuring customer satisfaction.

Innovation and R&D: Assess your commitment to innovation and research and development (R&D). Are you continually exploring new technologies, materials, or design concepts to stay ahead of the curve? Highlight any innovative product features or patents that showcase your brand's forward-thinking approach.

By identifying and leveraging your unique strengths, you can establish a strong USP that differentiates your brand in the bathroom fittings industry. Emphasize these strengths in your marketing messages, product positioning, and customer interactions. Align your branding strategies to highlight the value proposition that sets you apart from competitors. Continuously invest in enhancing your strengths and addressing any areas for improvement to maintain a competitive advantage in the market.

Determine Your Value Proposition

Based on the analysis of your competitors, target market, and unique strengths, determine your brand's value proposition. It should clearly articulate the unique benefits and value that your brand delivers to customers. Focus on the aspects that resonate most with your target market and address their pain points effectively. Your value proposition is the unique combination of benefits, value, and advantages that your brand offers to customers. It communicates why customers should choose your brand over competitors. Here are some key aspects to consider when determining your value proposition:

Benefits and Features: Identify the specific benefits and features that your bathroom fittings offer to customers. These could include water efficiency, durability, ease of installation, innovative designs, enhanced functionality, or customization options. Determine how these benefits address customer needs and deliver value.

Competitive Advantage: Assess the advantages you have over your competitors. This could include factors such as superior quality, extensive product range, faster delivery times, exceptional customer service, or competitive pricing. Identify what sets you apart and how it benefits customers.

Customer Needs Alignment: Understand the needs and pain points of your target customers. Determine how your products address those needs and provide solutions. Your value proposition should align with what your customers value most and emphasize the unique benefits they will gain by choosing your brand.

Emotional Appeal: Consider the emotional connection your brand can create with customers. How does your brand evoke positive emotions such as trust, reliability, luxury, or sustainability? Highlight the emotional benefits customers can experience by choosing your bathroom fittings.

Pricing Strategy: Determine how your pricing strategy aligns with your value proposition. If you position your brand as offering premium quality or unique features, a higher price point may be justified. Alternatively, if you aim to provide affordable options, emphasize the value for money your products offer.

Brand Personality: Define the personality and voice of your brand. Are you innovative, trustworthy, eco-conscious, or design-oriented? Your value proposition should reflect the personality and values that resonate with your target customers.

Differentiation: Identify the aspects that differentiate your brand from competitors. This could be related to design, sustainability initiatives, technological advancements, customer-centricity, or any other factors that make you unique. Highlight these differentiators in your value proposition.

Clear Communication: Craft a clear and concise value proposition statement that communicates the unique benefits customers can expect from your brand. This statement should be customer-focused and easy to understand. Use it consistently across your marketing materials to reinforce your brand's value.

By determining your value proposition, you can clearly articulate the unique benefits and advantages your brand offers in the bathroom fittings industry. This helps customers understand why they should choose your brand and creates a compelling reason for them to do business with you. Continuously evaluate and refine your value proposition based on customer feedback, market trends, and competitive landscape to ensure it remains relevant and impactful.

Highlight Differentiating Factors

Identify the specific features, attributes, or benefits that differentiate your brand from competitors. These could be factors like superior craftsmanship, innovative design, eco-friendly materials, extensive product customization options, or exceptional customer service. Emphasize these differentiating factors in your messaging so that you can position your brand as distinct and superior in the minds of customers. Here are some ways to highlight your differentiating factors:

Design Innovation: Emphasize any innovative designs or unique aesthetics that set your bathroom fittings apart. Whether it's sleek and contemporary styles, vintage-inspired designs, or cutting-edge technology integration, showcasing your design innovation can capture the attention of customers who seek distinctive and visually appealing products.

Quality and Craftsmanship: Highlight the superior quality and craftsmanship of your bathroom fittings. This could include using high-grade materials, employing skilled artisans, and implementing stringent quality control processes. Communicate the attention to detail and durability of your products, which can establish trust and credibility among customers.

Sustainable Practices: If your brand is committed to sustainability, emphasize your eco-friendly practices and initiatives. This could include using recycled materials, promoting water conservation features, or implementing environmentally responsible manufacturing processes. Highlighting your commitment to sustainability can attract environmentally conscious customers who prioritize eco-friendly options.

Customization Options: If your brand offers customization options for bathroom fittings, make sure to showcase this as a unique differentiating factor. Whether it's personalized finishes, tailored sizing, or modular components that allow customers to create their desired configurations, customization options can cater to individual preferences and provide a sense of exclusivity.

Technological Advancements: If your bathroom fittings incorporate advanced technologies, highlight these features as differentiators. This could include smart home integration, touchless operation, water-saving sensors, or innovative showering experiences. Showcasing your brand's technological advancements can appeal to customers who seek convenience, efficiency, and the latest innovations in their bathroom products.

Exceptional Customer Service: Differentiate your brand by providing exceptional customer service throughout the buying process and beyond. This includes responsive communication, knowledgeable support staff, and efficient after-sales service. By prioritizing customer satisfaction and building strong relationships, you can establish a positive reputation and differentiate yourself from competitors.

Industry Expertise: Highlight any industry expertise or specialized knowledge your brand possesses. This can include collaborations with renowned designers, partnerships with industry professionals, or participation in industry events and exhibitions. Positioning your brand as an expert in the bathroom fittings industry can instil confidence in customers and differentiate you from less established competitors.

Brand Heritage and Reputation: If your brand has a long-standing heritage or a strong reputation in the industry, leverage this as a differentiating factor. Communicate your brand's history, achievements, and positive customer experiences to build trust and credibility. Establishing yourself as a reputable and reliable brand can make customers choose you over newer or lesser-known competitors.

By highlighting your differentiating factors, you can create a compelling reason for customers to choose your brand in the bathroom fittings industry. Focus on what makes you unique, emphasize these qualities in your marketing materials and brand messaging, and consistently deliver on your promises. Continuously monitor the market and adapt your differentiating factors to stay ahead of competitors and meet evolving customer needs.

Communicate A Clear Message

Effective communication is essential in conveying your brand's value proposition and differentiating factors to your target audience in the bathroom fittings industry. Craft a clear and concise message that communicates your USP effectively. This message should resonate with your target market and highlight the unique value your brand offers. Use compelling language, visuals, and storytelling techniques to create an emotional connection with your audience. To effectively communicate a clear message, consider the following strategies:

Define Your Brand Identity: Start by clearly defining your brand identity, including your mission, vision, and core values. This will serve as the foundation for crafting a clear and consistent message. Understand what your brand stands for and what it aims to deliver to customers.

Identify Key Messaging Points: Identify the key messaging points that encapsulate your brand's unique selling proposition and differentiating factors. These messaging points should be concise, memorable, and aligned with your target market's needs and preferences. Focus on the aspects of your brand that resonate most with your audience and highlight them in your communication.

Develop a Brand Story: A brand story helps create an emotional connection with your audience. Develop a compelling narrative that communicates your brand's journey, values, and why it exists. The story should be authentic, engaging, and aligned with your target market's aspirations and desires. Use storytelling techniques to make your brand relatable and memorable.

Tailor Your Message to Different Channels: Adapt your message to different communication channels, such as your website, social media platforms, advertisements, and customer interactions. Each channel requires a unique approach, tone, and format. Ensure consistency in your messaging across all channels while adapting it to suit the specific context and requirements of each platform.

Use Clear and Simple Language: Avoid using jargon or technical terms that may confuse or alienate your audience. Use clear and simple language that is easy to understand. Communicate the benefits and value of your bathroom fittings in a way that is relatable and accessible to your target market.

Emphasize the Benefits: Clearly communicate the benefits that customers can expect from choosing your bathroom fittings. Highlight how your products solve their pain points, enhance their lifestyle, or meet their specific needs. Focus on the unique advantages and value they will gain from selecting your brand over competitors.

Consistency is Key: Consistency in messaging is crucial for brand recognition and building trust. Ensure that your message remains consistent across all touchpoints and interactions. Consistency helps reinforce your brand's image and allows customers to develop a clear understanding of what your brand stands for.

Visual Communication: Visual elements play a significant role in brand communication. Utilize visually appealing graphics, images, and videos that align with your brand's identity and message. Visuals can help convey your brand's personality, showcase product features, and create a memorable impression on your audience.

Listen and Respond: Communication is a two-way process. Actively listen to your customers' feedback, queries, and concerns. Respond promptly and empathetically, addressing their needs and providing solutions. Engage in meaningful conversations with your audience to build trust and loyalty.

Measure and Adapt: Continuously measure the effectiveness of your communication efforts. Monitor customer responses, engagement metrics, and market trends. Analyse the impact of your messaging and make necessary adjustments to improve your communication strategy.

By effectively communicating a clear message, you can create brand awareness, attract your target audience, and differentiate yourself in the competitive bathroom fittings industry. Consistent, compelling, and customer-centric messaging will help establish your brand's reputation, drive customer loyalty, and contribute to your overall success.

Consistency Across Brand Touchpoints

Consistency across brand touchpoints is crucial for building a strong and recognizable brand in the bathroom fittings industry. It ensures that your brand message, values, and visual identity are consistently presented to customers across various interactions and channels. Ensure consistency in delivering your USP across all brand touchpoints. This includes your website, marketing materials, packaging, social media presence, and customer interactions. Consistent messaging and brand experience will reinforce your USP and build brand recognition. Here are some key considerations for maintaining consistency across brand touchpoints:

Visual Identity: Establish a cohesive visual identity for your brand, including the logo, colour palette, typography, and graphic elements. Use these visual elements consistently across all touchpoints, including your website, packaging, marketing materials, social media profiles, and physical stores. Consistency in visual identity creates a sense of familiarity and helps customers recognize and associate your brand with its unique characteristics.

Tone and Voice: Define a consistent tone and voice for your brand's communication. Whether it's formal, casual, friendly, or authoritative, ensure that the tone remains consistent across all touchpoints. This includes website copy, social media posts, customer service interactions, and advertising campaigns. Consistency in tone and voice helps to build a strong brand personality and establishes a cohesive brand image.

Messaging: Develop consistent messaging that aligns with your brand values and key differentiators. Clearly define your brand's key messages and ensure they are consistently communicated across all touchpoints. Whether it's through advertising, product descriptions, social media content, or customer communications, your messaging should reinforce your brand's unique selling proposition and resonate with your target audience.

Customer Experience: Consistency in the customer experience is essential for building trust and loyalty. Ensure that the experience customers have with your brand is consistent across different touchpoints, such as online interactions, in-store visits, product packaging, and post-purchase support. Consistent delivery of high-quality products, prompt customer service, and seamless interactions contribute to a positive and reliable brand perception.

Brand Guidelines: Establish clear brand guidelines that

outline the standards for consistency across all touchpoints. These guidelines should cover elements such as logo usage, colour specifications, typography, imagery, and language guidelines. Provide these guidelines to all stakeholders, including marketing teams, designers, content creators, and external partners, to ensure that everyone understands and adheres to the brand's consistency standards.

Employee Training: Train your employees on the importance of maintaining brand consistency and provide them with the tools and resources they need to do so. Educate them on the brand's values, messaging, and visual identity, and emphasize the role they play in upholding the brand's consistency across customer interactions. Consistency in employee behaviour and communication helps to reinforce the brand's image and enhances the overall customer experience.

Regular Audits and Monitoring: Conduct regular audits and monitoring to ensure that brand consistency is maintained across all touchpoints. Regularly review your website, social media channels, advertising materials, packaging, and other customer-facing assets to identify any inconsistencies or deviations from the brand guidelines. Address any issues promptly and make necessary adjustments to maintain brand consistency.

By maintaining consistency across brand touchpoints, you create a cohesive and unified brand experience for your customers. This consistency builds trust, reinforces brand recognition, and enhances the overall perception of your brand in the bathroom fittings industry. Consistency establishes your brand as reliable, professional, and committed to delivering a seamless and memorable experience for your customers.

Monitor and Refine

Monitoring and refining your brand strategy is an ongoing process that allows you to adapt to changes in the market, customer preferences, and industry trends. It involves continuously evaluating the effectiveness of your branding efforts and making adjustments as needed to ensure your brand remains relevant and competitive in the bathroom fittings industry. You need to continuously monitor the market, industry trends, and customer feedback. Keep an eye on your competitors' activities and adapt as needed. Refine your USP over time based on evolving customer needs and market dynamics. Stay agile and responsive to maintain a competitive edge. Here are key aspects to consider when monitoring and refining your brand strategy:

Performance Metrics: Establish key performance indicators (KPIs) to measure the success of your branding initiatives. These could include metrics such as brand awareness, customer satisfaction, sales growth, market share, and customer loyalty. Regularly track and analyse these metrics to gain insights into the performance of your brand and identify areas that require improvement or adjustment.

Customer Feedback: Collect feedback from customers through surveys, focus groups, reviews, and social media interactions. Pay attention to their perceptions, preferences, and suggestions regarding your brand. This valuable feedback can help you understand how well your brand is resonating with your target market and identify opportunities for improvement.

Competitive Analysis: Keep a close eye on your competitors and monitor their branding strategies. Analyse their messaging, positioning, visual identity, and customer engagement tactics.

By understanding how your competitors are positioning themselves in the market, you can identify opportunities to differentiate your brand and refine your own branding strategy accordingly.

Industry Trends: Stay updated on the latest trends and innovations in the bathroom fittings industry. Monitor changes in consumer behaviour, emerging technologies, design trends, and sustainability practices. This knowledge can guide you in adapting your brand strategy to align with current industry dynamics and customer expectations.

Brand Audits: Conduct periodic brand audits to assess the consistency and effectiveness of your brand across all touchpoints. Evaluate how well your brand elements (logo, colour palette, typography) align with your brand positioning and target audience. Review your marketing materials, website, social media presence, and other customer-facing assets to ensure they reflect your brand identity and convey a cohesive message.

Brand Alignment: Regularly assess whether your brand is aligned with your business goals, values, and target market. Ensure that your brand positioning, messaging, and visual identity are consistent with the image you want to portray and the customers you want to attract. If any misalignments are identified, take steps to realign your brand strategy to better reflect your business objectives and resonate with your target market.

Continuous Improvement: Use the insights gained from monitoring and feedback to refine your brand strategy. Make adjustments to your messaging, visual identity, customer experience, or marketing tactics to enhance the effectiveness and impact of your brand. Embrace a mindset of continuous improvement and be willing to evolve your brand strategy to stay relevant in the ever-changing bathroom fittings industry.

By actively monitoring and refining your brand strategy, you can ensure that your brand remains fresh, competitive, and resonates with your target audience. This ongoing process allows you to adapt to market dynamics, meet customer expectations, and maintain a strong brand presence in the bathroom fittings industry. Regular monitoring and refinement enable you to make informed decisions and optimize your brand's performance to drive growth and success.

How CERA became a preferred brand of the Bathroom Fittings Industry in India?

CERA had a vision to revolutionise the way people perceive and experience bathroom fittings. They recognised the need to establish a unique selling proposition (USP) that would set them apart from their competitors and capture the attention of customers.

The journey to create their USP began with a deep understanding of their target market. CERA conducted extensive market research, studying the preferences, needs, and aspirations of their customers. They discovered that customers were seeking more than just functional bathroom fittings; they desired a luxurious and elegant experience that would transform their bathrooms into personal sanctuaries.

Armed with this valuable insight, CERA embarked on a mission to develop bathroom fittings that combined both style and functionality. They assembled a team of talented designers, engineers, and craftsmen who shared a passion for innovation and excellence. Together, they set out to create a product range that would elevate bathroom aesthetics and deliver exceptional performance.

CERA's commitment to quality and innovation led them to embrace cutting-edge technologies and materials. They invested in advanced manufacturing processes and rigorous quality control measures to ensure that every product bearing the CERA name would meet the highest standards of durability and performance. Their attention to detail and obsession with quality became a hallmark of the brand.

As CERA introduced their new line of bathroom fittings, they focused on highlighting the differentiating factors that set them apart. They emphasized the exquisite designs, superior craftsmanship, and meticulous attention to detail that went into each product. They communicated their USP through captivating marketing campaigns, showcasing the elegance and luxury that customers could expect from CERA fittings.

The response from the market was remarkable. Customers were captivated by the unique blend of aesthetics and functionality offered by CERA's bathroom fittings. The brand quickly gained recognition for its commitment to delivering premium products that transformed bathrooms into spaces of beauty and indulgence.

But CERA didn't stop there. They understood the importance of consistent brand communication and customer engagement. They built a strong network of authorized dealers and showrooms across the country, providing customers with a personalized and immersive experience. They invested in customer service training to ensure that every interaction with CERA was memorable and delightful.

Over time, CERA's USP became synonymous with luxury, innovation, and reliability in the bathroom fitting industry. Their commitment to delivering an unparalleled customer experience and their relentless pursuit of excellence positioned them as a trusted and aspirational brand.

As CERA's USP continued to resonate with customers, their market share grew steadily. They expanded their product portfolio to cater to diverse customer needs, offering a comprehensive range of bathroom fittings and accessories. CERA's success story served as an inspiration for other brands in the industry, encouraging them to rethink their own strategies and strive for uniqueness.

In conclusion, CERA Sanitaryware's journey to create their USP in the bathroom fitting industry was driven by a deep understanding of customer preferences, a relentless pursuit of innovation and quality, and a commitment to delivering a luxurious and transformative experience. Their dedication to their USP catapulted them to the forefront of the industry, earning them the trust and admiration of customers nationwide. CERA's story serves as a testament to the power of a well-defined USP in carving a distinctive identity and achieving success in the competitive bathroom fitting market.

CHAPTER 05

CRAFTING YOUR BRAND IDENTITY

Discussing the elements of a brand identity, including name, logo, colour scheme, and tone of voice

In the dynamic world of the bathroom fittings industry, creating a strong brand identity is paramount to establishing a memorable and recognizable presence. A well-crafted brand identity encompasses various elements that work harmoniously to convey the essence and values of your brand. This chapter defines the key components of a brand identity, including the name, logo, colour scheme, and tone of voice, and explores how they contribute to shaping your brand's image and perception.

The Power of a Name

When it comes to building a strong brand identity in the bathroom fittings industry, the power of a name cannot be underestimated. Your brand's name serves as the foundation upon which all other brand elements are built. It is the first point of contact for potential customers and sets the tone for their initial perception of your brand. The name of your brand plays a pivotal role in capturing attention and leaving a lasting impression. It should be unique, easy to pronounce, and reflective of your brand's personality and positioning. A carefully chosen name can evoke emotions, convey a sense of credibility, and differentiate your brand from competitors. Whether it's a name that embodies elegance and sophistication or one that exudes innovation and modernity, the right name can become a powerful asset in building your brand identity. Here are some key considerations when harnessing the power of a name:

Uniqueness: A distinctive and unique name is essential for standing out in a crowded marketplace. It should differentiate your brand from competitors and make it easily identifiable. Avoid generic or common names that may get lost in the sea of similar brands. Instead, strive for a name that is memorable and instantly recognizable.

Reflective of Brand Personality: Your brand's name should align with its personality and values. Consider the qualities and characteristics you want your brand to embody, whether it's luxury, innovation, sustainability, or reliability. The name should evoke the desired emotions and associations that resonate with your target audience.

Easy to Pronounce and Spell: A name that is easy to pronounce and spell helps facilitate word-of-mouth recommendations and makes it effortless for customers to find and remember your brand. Complex or confusing names can create barriers to communication and hinder brand recognition.

Scalability and Adaptability: Consider the long-term potential of your brand when choosing a name. Will it still be relevant and suitable as your brand expands or diversifies its product offerings? Ensure the name has the flexibility to accommodate future growth and evolution.

Cultural and Language Considerations: If your brand operates in different countries or targets diverse markets, be mindful of cultural and language nuances. Ensure that the name does not have any negative connotations or misinterpretations in different languages or cultures.

Legal Considerations: Conduct thorough research to ensure the availability of the chosen name and avoid any potential trademark or copyright infringements. Consult with legal professionals to protect your brand's name and secure the necessary intellectual property rights.

By understanding the significance of a name and carefully considering its implications, you can harness the power of a name to establish a distinctive and compelling brand identity in the bathroom fittings industry. The power of a well-crafted name extends beyond just being a label. It becomes an integral part of your brand's identity and can create a strong emotional connection with customers. A memorable and impactful name has the potential to become a valuable asset, contributing to brand recognition, recall, and loyalty.

Designing A Striking Logo

Your logo serves as the visual representation of your brand and is often the first element that customers encounter. It should be visually appealing, easily recognizable, and aligned with your brand's values and positioning. A well-designed logo combines elements such as typography, symbols, and colours to create a cohesive and memorable visual identity. It should evoke the desired emotions and impressions associated with your brand, effectively communicating your brand's essence at a glance. It is the face of your brand and plays a significant role in shaping the perception of your business. Here are key considerations when designing a striking logo:

Simplicity: A striking logo should be simple and easily recognizable. Avoid cluttered designs or intricate details that can be confusing or difficult to interpret. Aim for a clean and minimalistic design that conveys your brand's essence in a visually appealing manner.

Relevance: Your logo should be relevant to the bathroom fittings industry and reflect the nature of your business. Incorporate elements or symbols that are associated with bathroom fittings, such as faucets, showers, or abstract shapes that evoke a sense of water, cleanliness, or functionality.

Distinctiveness: To stand out from competitors, your logo should have a unique and distinctive design. Consider innovative ways to represent your brand while maintaining a sense of originality. It should be memorable and instantly recognizable, leaving a lasting impression on customers.

Colour Scheme: Choose a colour scheme that aligns with your brand's personality and evokes the desired emotions. Consider the psychology of colours and their associations. For example, blue can signify trust and reliability, while green can represent sustainability and freshness. Ensure the colours chosen are visually appealing and work well together.

Scalability: Your logo should be versatile and scalable to various sizes and formats. It should look equally appealing whether displayed on a small product packaging or a large billboard. Test your logo across different mediums to ensure its readability and visual impact.

Timelessness: Aim for a logo design that transcends trends and remains relevant over time. Avoid overly trendy elements that may become outdated quickly. A timeless logo design ensures longevity and consistency in brand recognition.

Professional Design: Invest in professional logo design services or work with a skilled graphic designer to create a high-quality logo. Professional designers have the expertise to translate your brand's identity into a visually striking and impactful logo. They can ensure the technical aspects, such as scalability and file formats, are properly addressed.

Remember, your logo will be present on all brand assets, including your website, product packaging, marketing materials, and digital platforms. It will become synonymous with your brand, so it is crucial to invest time and effort into designing a striking logo that captures the essence of your brand and resonates with your target audience. By carefully considering all the above aspects you can create a visually striking and memorable brand identity that sets your bathroom fittings business apart from competitors and leaves a lasting impression on customers.

Colours that Speak Volumes

Colour plays a significant role in shaping perceptions and triggering emotional responses. Choosing a colour scheme that resonates with your brand's personality and target audience is essential. Different colours evoke different emotions and associations. For instance, serene blues may convey a sense of calm and relaxation, while vibrant oranges may evoke energy and enthusiasm. Consistency in colour usage across all brand touchpoints reinforces brand recognition and creates a sense of cohesiveness. Here's an elaboration on the importance of colours in brand identity:

Understand Colour Psychology: Colours have psychological effects on people and can influence their perceptions and emotions. It is crucial to understand the meanings and associations commonly associated with different colours. For example, blue is often associated with trust, reliability, and calmness, while green represents freshness, growth, and sustainability. Consider the emotions and messages you want to convey through your brand and select colours that align with those intentions.

Consistency and Coherence: A well-defined colour scheme creates consistency and coherence across all brand touchpoints, including your logo, website, packaging, and marketing materials. Consistent use of colours reinforces brand recognition and helps customers associate specific colours with your brand. Select a primary colour or a combination of colours that best reflect your brand's personality, values, and target audience.

Cultural and Contextual Considerations: Keep in mind that colours can have different meanings and associations across cultures. If your bathroom fittings business operates in multiple regions or targets a diverse audience, consider the cultural context and ensure your chosen colours are culturally appropriate and resonate with the local audience. Conduct thorough research or seek advice from local experts to avoid any cultural misinterpretations or misunderstandings.

Differentiate from Competitors: Your colour scheme can

be a powerful tool for differentiation in a competitive market. Analyse the colours commonly used by your competitors and aim to stand out by selecting colours that set your brand apart. Find a unique combination or shade that represents your brand's distinct personality and creates a memorable visual identity.

Versatility and Accessibility: Consider the practical aspects of colour selection, such as the versatility of your chosen colours across different platforms and mediums. Ensure your colours work well in both digital and print formats and are easily visible and readable. Consider accessibility guidelines and ensure your colour choices provide sufficient contrast for individuals with visual impairments.

Test and Iterate: It's essential to test the effectiveness of your chosen colours by seeking feedback from your target audience or conducting market research. Monitor how your colours are perceived and adjust if necessary. Keep an eye on industry trends and evolving consumer preferences to ensure your colour scheme remains relevant and resonates with your target market.

Remember, colours are a powerful visual language that can communicate your brand's personality, evoke emotions, and create a memorable brand identity. By understanding colour psychology, maintaining consistency, considering cultural and contextual factors, differentiating from competitors, ensuring versatility and accessibility, and testing and iterating, you can create a colour scheme that speaks volumes and strengthens your brand's visual impact in the bathroom fittings industry.

Establishing a Distinctive Tone of Voice

Establishing a distinctive tone of voice is a crucial element in crafting your brand identity in the bathroom fittings industry. It involves defining the personality, language, and communication style that your brand will use to engage with your target audience. The tone of voice used in your brand's communications, including marketing materials, website content, and social media posts, is crucial in creating a consistent and authentic brand identity. It should align with your brand's values, target audience, and positioning. Whether it's a friendly and conversational tone, a formal and professional tone, or a playful and creative tone, the choice of language and communication style should reflect your brand's personality and resonate with your audience. Here's an elaboration on the importance of establishing a distinctive tone of voice:

Reflect Your Brand's Personality: Your brand's tone of voice should align with your brand's personality and values. Consider the attributes you want to convey, such as being professional, friendly, innovative, or authoritative. Think about how you want your brand to be perceived by your audience and ensure your tone of voice reflects those qualities consistently.

Understand Your Target Audience: To establish an effective tone of voice, you must have a deep understanding of your target audience. Consider their demographics, preferences, and communication styles. Tailor your tone of voice to resonate with your audience, whether they are homeowners, architects, interior designers, or contractors. Speak in a language and style that resonates with their needs, aspirations, and preferences.

Consistency and Authenticity: Consistency is key when it comes to establishing a tone of voice. Ensure that your brand's communication across different channels, including website content, social media posts, product descriptions, and customer interactions, remains consistent. This consistency helps build brand recognition and trust. Be authentic in your tone of voice and avoid trying to mimic or imitate other brands. Find a unique voice that reflects your brand's values and resonates with your audience.

Tailor Communication to Different Platforms: Different communication platforms may require slight adjustments in your tone of voice. While maintaining consistency, adapt your communication style to suit the specific platform and its audience. For instance, your tone may be more conversational on social media platforms like Instagram, while it may be more formal and informative on your website or in technical product documentation.

Use Language and Vocabulary Appropriately: Choose words and language that are in line with your brand's positioning and the preferences of your target audience. Consider industry-specific terminology and jargon that your audience may be familiar with. Strive for clarity and simplicity in your communication, avoiding overly complex or technical language that may alienate or confuse your audience.

Inject Personality and Emotion: Your tone of voice should go beyond just providing information; it should evoke emotions and connect with your audience on a deeper level. Inject personality, humour, or storytelling elements where appropriate to create a more engaging and memorable brand experience. However, ensure that the tone remains appropriate for your industry and the context of your communication.

Monitor and Adapt: Keep a pulse on how your audience responds to your brand's tone of voice. Monitor engagement, feedback, and customer interactions to gauge the effectiveness of your communication style. Be open to feedback and willing to adapt your tone of voice as needed to better connect with your audience and meet their evolving expectations.

Establishing a distinctive tone of voice helps your brand stand out, build relationships with your audience, and create a cohesive and memorable brand experience. By reflecting your brand's personality, understanding your target audience, maintaining consistency, being authentic, tailoring communication to different platforms, using appropriate language, injecting personality and emotion, and monitoring and adapting, you can establish a tone of voice that resonates with your audience and strengthens your brand's identity in the bathroom fittings industry. By incorporating these key elements—name, logo, colour scheme, and tone of voice—you can create a cohesive and impactful brand identity that sets you apart from competitors and resonates with customers.

Throughout this chapter, you'll explore practical strategies and examples of successful brand identities in the bathroom fittings industry. By understanding the importance of each element and how they work together, you'll gain insights into how to develop a brand identity that effectively communicates your brand's values, appeals to your target audience, and establishes a strong and memorable presence in the market.

Remember, a well-crafted brand identity is not static but evolves over time as your brand grows and adapts to changing market trends and customer expectations. Continuously evaluate and refine your brand identity to ensure it remains relevant, resonates with your audience, and strengthens your position in the competitive landscape of the bathroom fittings industry.

CHAPTER 06

BUILDING BRAND AWARENESS

Strategies for increasing visibility and recognition of your brand in the market

Building brand awareness is essential for the success of any business in the bathroom fittings industry. It involves creating familiarity and recognition among your target audience, establishing your brand as a trusted and reputable choice. In this chapter, we will explore various strategies that can help increase the visibility and recognition of your brand in the market.

Define Your Brand Identity

Defining your brand identity is a fundamental step in building brand awareness. It involves crafting a clear and cohesive representation of your brand's values, mission, personality, and unique selling proposition (USP). Before implementing any brand awareness strategies, it is crucial to have a clear understanding of your brand identity. This will guide your efforts and ensure consistency in all brand communication. When you define your brand identity, you establish the foundation upon which all other brand-related activities and strategies will be built. Here are some key aspects to consider when defining your brand identity:

Understand Your Target Audience: Start by gaining a deep understanding of your target audience. Identify their needs, preferences, values, and aspirations. This knowledge will help you tailor your brand identity to resonate with your audience and differentiate yourself from competitors.

Core Values and Mission: Determine the core values that guide your brand and the overarching mission that drives your business. Your values reflect what your brand stands for and how you conduct business, while your mission outlines the purpose and goals of your brand.

Unique Selling Proposition (USP): Identify what sets your brand apart from competitors and makes it unique. This could be a specific product feature, superior quality, innovative design, exceptional customer service, or any other aspect that differentiates your brand in the bathroom fittings industry.

Brand Personality: Define the personality traits and characteristics that embody your brand. Is your brand modern and sleek, traditional and reliable, or eco-friendly and sustainable? This helps establish an emotional connection with your audience and influences their perception of your brand.

Brand Story: Craft a compelling brand story that communicates your brand's history, values, and journey. Your brand story should be authentic, engaging, and resonate with your target audience. It helps create a deeper connection and builds trust with your customers.

Brand Voice: Determine the tone and language that aligns with your brand's personality and resonates with your target audience. Whether it's casual and friendly, formal and professional, or playful and creative, consistency in your brand voice across all communication channels helps build recognition and reinforces your brand identity.

Visual Identity: Establish a visually appealing and consistent brand identity through the use of a logo, typography, colour palette, and visual elements. Your logo should be distinct and memorable, while the choice of colours and typography should evoke the desired emotions and reflect your brand's personality.

Brand Guidelines: Develop brand guidelines that outline the rules and standards for using your brand assets consistently across all platforms and touchpoints. This includes guidelines for logo usage, typography, colours, imagery, and other visual elements. Consistency in branding elements helps reinforce brand recognition and build trust.

By defining your brand identity, you create a solid foundation for your brand's positioning and communication strategies. It ensures that every interaction with your brand aligns with your values, resonates with your target audience, and conveys a consistent brand message. This clarity in brand identity allows you to build strong brand awareness and recognition in the bathroom fittings industry.

Develop a Strong Visual Identity

Visual elements play a significant role in building brand awareness and brand recognition. Create a visually appealing and memorable logo, select a colour palette that represents your brand's personality, and choose fonts that align with your brand's tone. A visually appealing and cohesive brand identity helps distinguish your brand from competitors and allows customers to recognize and connect with your brand easily. Consistency in visual elements across all platforms and marketing materials will help reinforce your brand identity. Here are key considerations when developing a strong visual identity:

Logo Design: Your logo is the centrepiece of your visual identity. It should be unique, memorable, and visually represent your brand's essence. Consider factors such as colour, typography, and imagery that align with your brand's personality and values. A well-designed logo creates instant brand recognition and serves as a visual symbol that represents your brand across various platforms.

Colour Palette: Choose a colour palette that reflects your brand's personality and resonates with your target audience. Colours evoke specific emotions and can help convey the desired message. Consider the psychology of colours and select a combination that aligns with your brand identity. Use these colours consistently across your branding materials, website, packaging, and other visual assets.

Typography: Select fonts that complement your brand's personality and are legible across different mediums. Typography plays a crucial role in conveying the tone and style of your brand. Whether it's a modern and clean typeface or a classic and elegant font, ensure consistency in typography across all brand communication to maintain a cohesive visual identity.

Imagery and Graphics: Choose imagery and graphics that align with your brand's values and appeal to your target audience. Use high-quality photographs, illustrations, or graphics that enhance your brand story and evoke the desired emotions. Consistency in the style and tone of imagery helps establish a recognizable visual identity.

Design Elements: Consider incorporating design elements that are unique to your brand. This could include patterns, textures, icons, or illustrations that enhance the visual appeal and reinforce your brand identity. These design elements should be consistent and cohesive across all brand materials and platforms.

Packaging Design: If applicable, design packaging that reflects your brand identity and stands out on shelves. Consider how the visual elements, colours, and logo are incorporated into the packaging design to create a strong brand presence. Thoughtful packaging design can make a lasting impression on customers and enhance brand recognition.

Website and Digital Assets: Ensure that your brand's visual identity is consistent across your website and digital assets. Use the same colour palette, typography, and design elements to create a seamless brand experience for visitors. A visually appealing and user-friendly website reinforces your brand identity and builds credibility.

Brand Style Guide: Develop a brand style guide that outlines the specifications and guidelines for your visual identity. This guide should include details about logo usage, colour codes, typography, imagery guidelines, and any other visual elements specific to your brand. A brand style guide ensures consistency and helps maintain a strong visual identity across different platforms and marketing materials.

By developing a strong visual identity, you create a cohesive and recognizable brand presence in the bathroom fittings industry. Consistency in visual elements across various touchpoints helps build brand awareness, enhances brand recall, and fosters a strong connection with your target audience. A visually appealing and well-defined brand identity sets the stage for effective brand communication and positioning.

Content Marketing

Content marketing is a powerful strategy for building brand awareness in the bathroom fittings industry. It involves creating and distributing valuable and relevant content to attract and engage your target audience. By providing informative, educational, and entertaining content, you establish your brand as a trusted authority in the industry and build a loyal following. Create valuable and relevant content that resonates with your target audience. Use blog posts, articles, videos, and infographics to educate, inspire, and engage your audience. Share your expertise and insights to position your brand as a thought leader in the industry. Here are key aspects to consider when implementing a content marketing strategy:

Targeted Audience: Identify your target audience and understand their needs, preferences, and pain points. Tailor your content to address their specific challenges and provide solutions that align with your brand's expertise. By delivering content that resonates with your audience, you can attract their attention and establish a connection.

Valuable and Relevant Content: Create content that offers value to your audience. This can include informative blog posts, how-to guides, educational videos, infographics, and industry insights. Share valuable tips, trends, and best practices related to bathroom fittings, installation, maintenance, and design. The goal is to position your brand as a go-to resource and build trust with your audience.

Consistency and Frequency: Consistency is key in content marketing. Develop a content calendar and establish a regular publishing schedule. This ensures that your audience receives fresh and engaging content on a consistent basis. By maintaining a consistent presence, you keep your brand top of mind and nurture a loyal following.

Visual Appeal: Make your content visually appealing by incorporating high-quality images, videos, and graphics. Visual elements enhance engagement and make your content more shareable on social media platforms. Utilize visual storytelling techniques to communicate your brand's message effectively and capture the attention of your audience.

SEO Optimization: Optimize your content for search engines to increase its visibility and reach. Conduct keyword research to identify relevant keywords and incorporate them naturally into your content. This helps improve your website's search engine rankings, making it easier for potential customers to discover your brand.

Social Media Promotion: Leverage social media platforms to amplify your content and reach a wider audience. Share your content on platforms like Facebook, Instagram, Twitter, and LinkedIn to engage with your followers and encourage social sharing. Encourage discussions, respond to comments, and build relationships with your audience through social media engagement.

Guest Blogging and Collaborations: Explore opportunities to contribute guest posts to industry blogs or collaborate with influencers and experts in the bathroom fittings industry. By leveraging their audience and credibility, you can expand your reach and gain exposure to a larger audience.

Analytics and Measurement: Track the performance of your content marketing efforts using analytics tools. Monitor metrics such as website traffic, engagement, social shares, and conversions to gain insights into the effectiveness of your content strategy. Use this data to refine and optimize your content approach for better results.

Content marketing allows you to showcase your brand's expertise, build trust with your audience, and establish a strong brand presence in the bathroom fittings industry. By consistently delivering valuable and relevant content, you can attract and engage your target audience, ultimately driving brand awareness, customer loyalty, and business growth.

Social Media Marketing

Social media marketing is an essential component of building brand awareness in the bathroom fittings industry. It involves utilizing social media platforms to promote your brand, engage with your audience, and create a strong online presence. Utilize popular social media platforms to connect with your audience and build brand awareness. Share compelling visuals, engage in conversations, and provide helpful information. Encourage user-generated content and leverage influencers to expand your reach. Here are key aspects to consider when implementing a social media marketing strategy:

Platform Selection: Identify the social media platforms that are most relevant to your target audience. Platforms like

Facebook, Instagram, Twitter, LinkedIn, and Pinterest offer various opportunities to showcase your brand and connect with potential customers. Understand the unique features and demographics of each platform to tailor your content and engagement strategies accordingly.

Consistent Branding: Maintain consistent branding across your social media profiles. Use your brand logo, colours, and visual elements in your profile pictures, cover photos, and posts. This helps in creating a cohesive and recognizable brand identity, reinforcing brand recall among your followers.

Engaging Content: Create and share compelling content that resonates with your audience. This can include product showcases, behind-the-scenes glimpses, design inspiration, installation guides, and customer testimonials. Encourage user-generated content by featuring customer photos and stories. Use visuals, such as high-quality images and videos, to grab attention and drive engagement.

Community Building: Foster a sense of community among your social media followers. Encourage conversations, respond to comments and messages promptly, and show genuine interest in your audience's opinions and feedback. By building meaningful connections with your followers, you can cultivate brand loyalty and advocacy.

Influencer Partnerships: Collaborate with influencers or industry experts who have a significant following in the bathroom fittings space. Partnering with influencers can help expand your reach, increase brand visibility, and tap into their credibility and expertise. Influencers can showcase your products, share their experiences, and promote your brand to their followers.

Paid Advertising: Consider utilizing paid social media advertising to reach a broader audience and enhance brand visibility. Platforms like Facebook and Instagram offer targeted advertising options that allow you to reach specific demographics, interests, and locations. Invest in sponsored posts, promoted content, and targeted ads to amplify your brand messaging.

Hashtag Campaigns: Create branded hashtags to encourage user-generated content and increase brand exposure. Encourage your audience to share their bathroom fittings-related experiences, designs, or installations using your branded hashtags. This not only generates user engagement but also helps in spreading your brand message organically.

Social Listening: Monitor social media conversations and stay informed about what people are saying about your brand, products, and competitors. Social listening allows you to address customer concerns, gather feedback, and identify opportunities for improvement. Engage in conversations, respond to mentions and reviews, and demonstrate your commitment to customer satisfaction.

Analytics and Measurement: Utilize social media analytics tools to track the performance of your social media marketing efforts. Monitor metrics such as reach, engagement, follower growth, click-through rates, and conversions. Analyse the data to gain insights into the effectiveness of your social media strategy and make data-driven decisions for improvement.

Social media marketing offers a powerful platform to build brand awareness, engage with your target audience, and drive business growth in the bathroom fittings industry. By leveraging the unique features and reach of social media platforms, you can connect with potential customers, foster brand loyalty, and position your brand as a leader in the industry.

Online Advertising

Online advertising plays a crucial role in building brand awareness and reaching a wider audience in the bathroom fittings industry. It involves strategically placing advertisements across various online platforms to promote your brand, products, and services. Invest in targeted online advertising campaigns to reach a broader audience. Use platforms like Google Ads and social media advertising to promote your brand and products to specific demographics and locations. Leverage retargeting strategies to stay top of mind with potential customers. Here are key aspects to consider when implementing online advertising strategies:

Targeted Advertising: Take advantage of targeted advertising options available on platforms such as Google Ads, social media platforms, and industry-specific websites. These platforms allow you to define specific demographics, interests, and geographic locations to ensure your ads reach the most relevant audience. Targeted advertising helps maximize the impact of your ad spend by focusing on potential customers who are more likely to be interested in your products.

Display Advertising: Utilize display advertising to showcase visually appealing ads on websites, blogs, and online publications that are relevant to the bathroom fittings industry. Display ads can be in the form of banners, images, or interactive media. Consider partnering with industry-specific websites or publications to reach a highly targeted audience and leverage their existing readership or viewership.

Search Engine Advertising: Implement search engine advertising, such as Google Ads, to appear at the top of search engine results when users search for relevant keywords related to bathroom fittings. This form of advertising allows you to target specific keywords, create compelling ad copy, and direct users to relevant landing pages on your website. It helps increase visibility, drive website traffic, and capture potential customers at the moment they are actively searching for bathroom fittings.

Remarketing: Implement remarketing campaigns to re-engage users who have previously visited your website or shown interest in your products. By placing cookies on their browsers, you can display targeted ads to these users as they browse other websites or platforms. Remarketing helps reinforce your brand, increase brand recall, and encourage users to revisit your website and make a purchase.

Video Advertising: Leverage the power of video advertising on platforms like YouTube to showcase your brand and products through engaging video content. Create informative and visually appealing videos that highlight the features, benefits, and installation processes of your bathroom fittings. Video ads allow you to capture the attention of your target audience, communicate your brand message effectively, and drive engagement.

Native Advertising: Consider native advertising, which involves creating content that seamlessly blends with the format and style of the platform where it appears. Native ads can be in the form of sponsored articles, recommended content, or product placements within relevant online publications or industry websites. Native advertising provides an opportunity to reach audiences in a non-intrusive manner and establish credibility by associating your brand with trusted content.

Mobile Advertising: With the increasing use of mobile devices, optimize your online advertising campaigns for mobile platforms. Ensure that your ads are mobile-friendly, load quickly, and provide a seamless user experience. Utilize mobile-specific ad formats, such as mobile banners or in-app ads, to effectively target users who primarily access the internet through their smartphones or tablets.

Ad Performance Tracking and Optimization: Regularly monitor the performance of your online advertising campaigns and make necessary optimizations to maximize their effectiveness. Track key metrics such as impressions, clicks, click-through rates, conversions, and return on investment (ROI). Analyse the data to identify trends, refine targeting, improve ad copy, and allocate budget to channels that deliver the best results.

Online advertising offers a wide range of opportunities to increase brand visibility, drive website traffic, and generate leads in the bathroom fittings industry. By strategically planning and executing online advertising campaigns, you can effectively reach your target audience, increase brand awareness, and position your brand as a trusted and preferred choice for bathroom fittings.

Collaborate with Influencers

In today's digital age, influencers have become powerful voices and trusted sources of information for consumers. Collaborating with influencers in the bathroom fittings industry can significantly boost your brand awareness and credibility. Partner with influential individuals or organizations in the bathroom fittings industry to promote your brand. This can include industry experts, interior designers, or popular social media influencers. Their endorsement can significantly increase brand visibility and credibility. Here's how you can effectively collaborate with influencers:

Identify Relevant Influencers: Research and identify influencers who have a strong following and influence in the bathroom fittings industry. Look for influencers who align with your brand values, target audience, and niche. Consider factors such as their engagement rates, audience demographics, and the authenticity of their content.

Build Relationships: Once you've identified potential influencers, start building relationships with them. Engage with their content by liking, commenting, and sharing their posts. This helps create familiarity and establishes a connection with the influencer. Reach out to them through direct messages or email to express your interest in collaborating.

Define Collaboration Objectives: Clearly define your collaboration objectives and what you aim to achieve through the partnership. It could be increasing brand visibility, generating product reviews, showcasing installations, or creating engaging content. Communicate your goals to the influencer so that they understand how they can best promote your brand.

Tailor Collaboration Ideas: Work closely with influencers to develop collaboration ideas that align with their style and resonate with their audience. This could include sponsored posts, product reviews, tutorials, giveaways, or engaging stories featuring your brand and products. Allow influencers creative freedom to showcase your bathroom fittings in an authentic and compelling way.

Provide Quality Products and Experiences: To ensure a successful collaboration, provide influencers with high-quality bathroom fittings products and memorable experiences. This allows them to genuinely experience and appreciate the quality, functionality, and design of your products. A positive experience will reflect in their content and recommendations to their audience.

Track and Measure Results: Monitor the performance of the influencer collaborations by tracking key metrics such as engagement rates, reach, impressions, website traffic, and conversions. Use trackable links or unique discount codes to attribute sales or leads generated through influencer campaigns. This data will help you assess the effectiveness of the collaborations and make informed decisions for future partnerships.

Long-Term Partnerships: Consider establishing long-term partnerships with influencers who consistently deliver positive results and align well with your brand. Building long-term relationships allows for continuity in brand messaging and provides an opportunity to create deeper connections with the influencer's audience over time.

Compliance and Transparency: Ensure compliance with relevant advertising regulations and guidelines when collaborating with influencers. Clearly communicate any sponsorship or partnership arrangements to maintain transparency with the audience. This helps build trust and credibility both for the influencer and your brand.

By collaborating with influencers in the bathroom fittings industry, you can tap into their engaged audience, leverage their expertise, and amplify your brand message. Influencers have the ability to showcase your products in an authentic and relatable manner, driving brand awareness and influencing purchasing decisions. Choose influencers strategically, nurture relationships, and track the impact of collaborations to maximize the benefits of influencer marketing for your brand.

Participate in Industry Events

Participating in industry events is an effective strategy for building brand awareness and establishing your presence in the bathroom fittings industry. These events provide valuable opportunities to connect with industry professionals, potential customers, and key stakeholders. Attend and exhibit at trade shows, exhibitions, and industry conferences to showcase your brand and connect with industry professionals and potential customers. Sponsor relevant events and participate in panel discussions or speaking engagements to establish your brand as a reputable authority. Here are some key aspects to consider when participating in industry events:

Research and Select Relevant Events: Identify industry events that attract your target audience and align with your brand objectives. This could include trade shows, exhibitions, conferences, and networking events specifically focused on the bathroom fittings industry. Research the reputation, size, and audience demographics of the events to ensure they are a good fit for your brand.

Plan Your Presence: Once you've selected the events to participate in, carefully plan your presence to maximize your impact. This includes designing an eye-catching booth or display area that reflects your brand identity. Consider incorporating interactive elements, product demonstrations, and informative materials to engage attendees. Create a cohesive visual identity using your brand colours, logo, and signage to enhance brand recognition.

Engage with Attendees: Actively engage with event attendees by initiating conversations, demonstrating your products, and sharing your brand story. Train your staff to be knowledgeable about your products and brand values so they can effectively communicate with potential customers and address their inquiries. Encourage attendees to leave their contact information for future follow-ups and lead generation.

Showcase Your Expertise: Position yourself as an industry expert by offering educational sessions, workshops, or presentations at the event. Share insights, trends, and valuable information related to bathroom fittings that attendees can benefit from. This helps establish credibility, builds trust, and positions your brand as a thought leader in the industry.

Collaborate with Industry Influencers: Leverage the presence of industry influencers or experts who are attending or speaking at the event. Engage in conversations with them, seek opportunities for collaborations or joint activities that can enhance your brand visibility and reach. Collaborating with influential individuals in the industry can help amplify your brand message and attract a wider audience.

Collect Feedback and Network: Take advantage of industry events to collect feedback from attendees, gather market insights, and understand customer preferences. Conduct surveys, encourage discussions, and actively listen to the needs and challenges of potential customers. Networking with industry professionals, suppliers, and potential business partners can also open doors to valuable connections and collaborations.

Follow-Up and Maintain Relationships: After the event, follow up with the contacts you made to nurture relationships and convert leads into customers. Send personalized emails, connect on social media, and share relevant content to stay on their radar. Maintaining relationships with industry contacts can lead to future collaborations, referrals, and partnerships that contribute to your brand's growth.

Participating in industry events provides a platform to showcase your brand, establish industry relationships, and gain valuable exposure. By strategically planning your presence, engaging with attendees, and leveraging the networking opportunities, you can enhance your brand awareness, generate leads, and stay ahead in the competitive bathroom fittings industry.

Public Relations

Public relations (PR) play a crucial role in building brand awareness and reputation in the bathroom fittings industry. It involves managing the communication between your brand and the public, including customers, industry professionals, media outlets, and stakeholders. Develop relationships with media outlets and industry publications to secure press coverage. Send out press releases for new product launches, partnerships, or company milestones. Positive media coverage can significantly enhance brand visibility and credibility. Here are key aspects to consider when implementing PR strategies:

Develop a PR Strategy: Start by defining your PR objectives and target audience. Identify the key messages you want to convey and the specific media outlets or platforms you want to target. Your PR strategy should align with your overall brand identity and business goals.

Media Relations: Build relationships with relevant journalists, reporters, and bloggers who cover the bathroom fittings industry. Send out press releases or media kits to announce new product launches, company news, or industry insights. Offer yourself or your brand executives as experts available for interviews or feature stories. Engage in media outreach to secure media coverage that increases your brand visibility.

Thought Leadership: Position yourself as a thought leader in the bathroom fittings industry by sharing valuable insights, trends, and expertise. Write articles or guest blog posts for industry publications, contribute to online forums, or speak at industry conferences. Establishing yourself as an authority helps build credibility and enhances your brand reputation.

Community Engagement: Engage with the community by supporting relevant causes, sponsoring industry events, or participating in charitable initiatives. This helps to build a positive image for your brand and showcases your commitment to social responsibility. Collaborate with local organizations, participate in community projects, and leverage PR opportunities around these activities.

Crisis Management: Develop a crisis management plan to handle any unforeseen issues or negative publicity. Proactively address customer concerns, respond to feedback, and communicate transparently during challenging situations. Having a well-defined crisis management strategy in place helps to protect your brand's reputation and maintain customer trust.

Awards and Recognitions: Apply for industry awards and recognitions that highlight your brand's achievements, innovations, and contributions to the bathroom fittings industry. Winning awards or being recognized as a top brand adds credibility and builds trust among customers and industry professionals.

Online Reputation Management: Monitor and manage your brand's online reputation through social media listening, review management, and proactive engagement. Respond promptly to customer feedback, address negative reviews or comments professionally, and highlight positive customer experiences. Online reputation management is essential for maintaining a positive brand image in the digital age.

Influencer Partnerships: Collaborate with influencers or industry experts who have a significant following and influence in the bathroom fittings industry. Engage them in promoting your brand, reviewing your products, or creating sponsored content. Influencer partnerships can amplify your brand message and reach a wider audience.

Effective PR strategies help generate positive publicity, enhance brand credibility, and increase brand awareness in the bathroom fittings industry. By leveraging media relations, thought leadership, community engagement, and online reputation management, you can establish a strong brand presence and build lasting relationships with your target audience.

Customer Referral Programs

Customer referral programs are an effective strategy for building brand awareness and generating new business in the bathroom fittings industry. By incentivizing your existing customers to refer their friends, family, or colleagues to your brand, you can tap into the power of word-of-mouth marketing. Encourage your satisfied customers to refer your brand to their friends and colleagues. Implement referral programs that reward customers for successful referrals. This can generate word-of-mouth marketing and increase brand awareness. Here are key elements to consider when implementing a customer referral program:

Define Referral Incentives: Determine what incentives you will offer to customers who refer new business to your brand. This could be in the form of discounts, rewards, exclusive promotions, or even cash incentives. The incentive should be attractive enough to motivate customers to actively participate in the referral program.

Clear Referral Process: Establish a simple and straightforward process for customers to refer others. Provide them with a unique referral code or link that they can share with their contacts. Ensure that the referral process is user-friendly and accessible through various channels, such as email, social media, or your website.

Promote the Referral Program: Create awareness about your referral program through various marketing channels. Utilize your website, social media platforms, email newsletters, and in-store signage to inform customers about the program and its benefits. Encourage them to spread the word and participate in the referral program.

Track and Reward Referrals: Implement a tracking system to monitor and measure the success of your customer referral program. Keep a record of referred customers and the customers who made the referrals. This allows you to identify and reward those customers who successfully bring in new business to your brand.

Personalize the Experience: Make the referral program a personalized experience for your customers. Send them personalized thank-you messages or exclusive offers for their referrals. This helps to strengthen the customer relationship and encourages continued participation in the program.

Monitor and Optimize: Continuously monitor the performance of your referral program and gather feedback from customers. Analyse the data to identify areas of improvement or potential bottlenecks. Make necessary adjustments and optimize the program to maximize its effectiveness.

Share Success Stories: Highlight success stories and testimonials from customers who have participated in your referral program. Share these stories through your marketing channels to inspire and motivate other customers to join in. Positive testimonials create social proof and enhance the credibility of your brand.

Provide Excellent Customer Experience: Ensure that every customer has a positive experience with your brand. Exceptional customer service, high-quality products, and prompt problem resolution are crucial for customer satisfaction. A satisfied customer is more likely to refer others to your brand.

By implementing a well-designed customer referral program, you can leverage the power of your existing customer base to expand your brand reach and attract new customers. A successful referral program not only helps in building brand awareness but also fosters customer loyalty and advocacy.

Monitor and Analyse

Monitoring and analysing the performance of your brand awareness strategies is essential to ensure their effectiveness and make informed decisions for improvement. Continuously monitor the effectiveness of your brand awareness strategies. Analyse website traffic, social media engagement, and conversion rates to measure the impact of your efforts. Make adjustments and refine your strategies based on the insights gained. Here are key steps to effectively monitor and analyse your brand awareness efforts:

Set Clear Objectives: Define specific goals and key performance indicators (KPIs) that align with your brand awareness strategies. These could include metrics such as website traffic, social media engagement, brand mentions, customer inquiries, or sales attributed to brand awareness efforts.

Utilize Analytics Tools: Use analytics tools such as Google Analytics, social media insights, or marketing automation platforms to gather data on the performance of your brand awareness initiatives. These tools provide valuable insights into user behaviour, engagement metrics, and audience demographics.

Track Key Metrics: Regularly track and analyse the key metrics associated with your brand awareness strategies. Monitor website traffic, bounce rates, time spent on page, social media followers, likes, comments, shares, reach, and engagement rates. Identify trends, patterns, and areas of improvement based on the data collected.

Conduct Surveys and Feedback: Seek feedback from your target audience through surveys, polls, or customer feedback forms. Gain insights into their awareness of your brand, perception, and recall. This qualitative data can provide valuable information about your brand's visibility and reputation.

Competitor Analysis: Monitor and analyse the activities and strategies of your competitors in the bathroom fittings industry. Identify areas where they are gaining visibility and recognition and assess how your brand compares. This analysis can help you identify new opportunities or adjust your own strategies accordingly.

Evaluate Return on Investment (ROI): Assess the ROI of your brand awareness efforts by comparing the cost of your initiatives with the results achieved. Calculate the impact on lead generation, customer acquisition, and revenue growth. This analysis helps determine the effectiveness and profitability of your brand awareness strategies.

Make Data-Driven Decisions: Use the insights gathered from monitoring and analysis to make data-driven decisions for optimizing your brand awareness strategies. Identify what is working well and replicate those successful tactics. Identify areas of improvement and adjust your approach to enhance effectiveness.

Continuously Improve: Regularly review and refine your brand awareness strategies based on the monitoring and analysis conducted. Experiment with new tactics, channels, or messaging based on the insights gained. Continuously strive to enhance your brand's visibility, recognition, and impact in the bathroom fittings industry.

Monitoring and analysing the performance of your brand awareness strategies allows you to identify strengths, weaknesses, and areas of improvement. It enables you to refine your approach, optimize your resources, and make informed decisions to enhance your brand's visibility and recognition in the market.

To sum up, building brand awareness requires a strategic and consistent approach. By defining your brand identity, developing a strong visual identity, implementing content marketing and social media strategies, leveraging online advertising, collaborating with influencers, participating in industry events, utilizing public relations, implementing customer referral programs, and monitoring and analysing your efforts, you can increase the visibility and recognition of your brand in the bathroom fittings industry. Building brand awareness sets the foundation for long-term success and establishes your brand as a trusted choice in the market.

CHAPTER 07

BRAND POSITIONING IN THE BATHROOM FITTINGS MARKET

How to position your brand effectively in the market to attract your target audience

In this Chapter we go deep inside into the critical aspect of brand positioning in the bathroom fittings market. Effective brand positioning allows you to establish a distinct identity and occupy a unique space in the minds of your target audience. It involves strategically differentiating your brand from competitors and creating a compelling perception that resonates with customers. Here are some key insights and strategies to help you position your brand effectively in the bathroom fittings market:

Define Your Target Market

To position your brand successfully, you must have a clear understanding of your target market. Identify the specific demographics, psychographics, and preferences of your ideal customers. This information will help you tailor your brand positioning and communication to align with their needs and aspirations.

Develop detailed buyer personas that represent different segments of your target market. A buyer persona is a fictional profile that represents a specific group of customers. Include demographic information, psychographics, interests, goals, challenges, and preferred communication channels for each persona. This exercise helps you visualize and understand the diverse needs and behaviours of your target audience.

Identify the pain points, challenges, and unmet needs of your target market. This will help you align your brand positioning and messaging to address these specific concerns. Conduct surveys, interviews, or focus groups to gather direct feedback from your target audience and gain deeper insights into their preferences and desires. Refine your target market definition based on the insights you have gathered. Test your assumptions and hypotheses through market testing, surveys, or pilot campaigns. Continuously gather feedback and data to refine your target market definition and ensure it aligns with the reality of your customers' preferences and behaviours.

Study your competitors' target market and positioning strategies. Identify gaps or underserved segments in the market that your brand can effectively target. Differentiate yourself by understanding the unique needs and desires of these untapped customer groups and tailor your brand positioning accordingly. Also, keep a pulse on the market dynamics and adapt your target market definition as needed. Consumer preferences and behaviours evolve over time, so it's important to stay updated and responsive to changes in the market. Regularly review and assess your target market definition to ensure it remains accurate and relevant.

By defining your target market effectively, you can tailor your brand positioning, messaging, and marketing efforts to resonate with the right audience. Understanding your target market's needs, preferences, and pain points will enable you to position your brand as the solution that meets their specific requirements, ultimately driving better brand positioning and business success.

Conduct Market Research

Conduct thorough market research to gain insights into the competitive landscape, customer preferences, and emerging trends. Analyse competitor offerings, pricing strategies, and marketing tactics. This research will enable you to identify gaps in the market and uncover opportunities for differentiation.

Start by clearly defining the objectives of your market research. Determine what specific information you want to gather, such as customer demographics, buying behaviours, preferences, competitor analysis, or market trends. Setting clear objectives will help you focus your research efforts. Choose the appropriate research methods to gather the required data. Common market research methods in the bathroom fittings industry include surveys, interviews, focus groups, observation, and online research. Each method has its strengths and limitations, so select the ones that best align with your research objectives and target audience.

Identify the specific target audience you want to study. This can be based on demographics, such as age, gender, location, or specific customer segments you wish to target. Ensure that your target audience is representative of your intended market to obtain accurate insights. Create the necessary research instruments, such as survey questionnaires, interview guides, or discussion protocols for focus groups. Design questions that elicit the information you need and consider using a mix of closed-ended and open-ended questions to gather quantitative and qualitative data.

Implement your chosen research methods to collect data from your target audience. This can involve distributing surveys online or offline, conducting interviews or focus groups, or observing customer behaviours in real-life or digital environments. Ensure that data collection methods are ethical, and privacy and confidentiality of respondents are respected. Once you have collected the data, analyse it to extract meaningful insights. Use statistical analysis tools to process quantitative data and identify patterns, trends, and correlations. For qualitative data, employ techniques such as thematic analysis or content analysis to identify recurring themes and derive qualitative insights.

Interpret the research findings to gain a deep understanding of customer preferences, market trends, and competitive dynamics. Look for key insights and patterns that can inform your brand positioning, product development, marketing strategies, and customer engagement initiatives. Use the research findings to make informed decisions about your brand positioning, marketing campaigns, product features, pricing strategies, and customer experience. Consider the identified opportunities and challenges in the bathroom fittings industry and align your business strategies accordingly.

Market research is an ongoing process. Continuously monitor and update your research to stay informed about evolving customer preferences, industry trends, and competitive landscape. Regularly conduct market research to ensure that your brand positioning remains relevant and effective. By conducting thorough market research in the bathroom fittings industry, you can gather valuable insights that will guide your brand positioning efforts, help you understand customer needs, and stay ahead of the competition. The research findings will enable you to make informed decisions that resonate with your target audience and contribute to the success of your business.

Identify Your Unique Value Proposition (UVP)

Determine what sets your brand apart from competitors and why customers should choose your bathroom fittings over others. Your UVP should highlight the unique benefits, features, or solutions your brand offers. Whether it's exceptional quality, innovative design, eco-friendly materials, or personalized customer service, your UVP should resonate with your target audience and differentiate your brand in a meaningful way.

Begin by gaining a deep understanding of your target audience. Identify their needs, pain points, and preferences when it comes to use of bathroom fittings. Conduct market research, analyse customer feedback, and study industry trends to gather insights into what matters most to your target audience. Conduct a thorough analysis of your competitors to identify gaps and opportunities in the market. Assess their offerings, pricing, marketing strategies, and customer feedback. Look for areas where you can differentiate your brand and provide unique value that competitors may be overlooking.

Determine your brand's core competencies and strengths. What sets your bathroom fittings apart from others in terms of quality, design, functionality, or innovation? Consider factors such as manufacturing processes, material selection, technology integration, or sustainability practices. Highlight the aspects that give your brand a competitive edge. Based on your understanding of your target audience and your brand's strengths, determine the specific benefits and solutions your bathroom fittings offer. How do they address customer pain points or fulfil customer desires? Consider aspects such as durability, water efficiency, ease of installation, aesthetics, maintenance, or customized solutions.

Once you have identified your unique value proposition and customer benefits, craft a clear and compelling message that communicates your brand's value to your target audience. Use simple, concise language that resonates with your customers. Focus on the key benefits and solutions your brand offers and articulate them in a way that captures attention and creates a strong impression.

Ensure consistency by integrating your unique value proposition across all brand touchpoints. This includes your website, marketing materials, packaging, customer interactions, and any other point of contact with your audience. Consistent messaging will reinforce your brand's value proposition and help create a strong brand identity. As the bathroom fittings industry evolves, continuously reassess your unique value proposition to stay relevant. Monitor industry trends, technological advancements, and changing customer preferences. Adapt and evolve your UVP to ensure it aligns with the evolving needs of your target audience.

By following all the above areas, you can identify and develop a unique value proposition for your bathroom fittings brand. Your UVP will differentiate your brand, communicate your distinct value to customers, and attract your target audience, helping you position your brand effectively in the market.

Develop a Brand Positioning Statement

Craft a concise and compelling brand positioning statement that encapsulates your brand's unique value and target audience. This statement should articulate the essence of your brand, its key differentiators, and the specific benefits it offers to customers. Use this statement as a guiding compass for all your brand communication and marketing efforts.

Example of a Brand Positioning Statement:

"At AquaD Bathware, we are dedicated to redefining the bathroom experience for modern homeowners. Our innovative and stylish range of bathroom fittings combines cutting-edge design, superior functionality, and unmatched durability. With a commitment to sustainable practices and using premium quality materials, we offer eco-friendly solutions that elevate both aesthetics and performance. Our mission is to create bathrooms that inspire and transform, providing our customers with the perfect blend of luxury and functionality. Choose AquaD Bathware for a truly exceptional bathing experience that reflects your discerning taste and enhances your everyday living."

Communicate Your Differentiators

Communicating your differentiators effectively is vital to the success of your brand in the competitive bathroom fittings industry. To effectively communicate your differentiators, start by identifying what sets your brand apart from the competition. This could be your unique product features, exceptional customer service, or sustainable manufacturing processes.

Once you have identified your differentiators, craft a clear and compelling message that highlights these unique qualities. Use various communication channels such as your website, social media platforms, advertising campaigns, and customer interactions to consistently deliver this message to your target audience. It is important to emphasize the value and benefits that your differentiators bring to customers, showcasing how they solve their pain points or meet their specific needs.

Use engaging visuals, persuasive language, and storytelling techniques to capture attention and make a lasting impression. Regularly evaluate and refine your communication strategies based on customer feedback and market trends to ensure that your brand's differentiators remain relevant and effectively communicated. By effectively communicating your differentiators, you can attract and engage your target audience, build brand loyalty, and gain a competitive edge in the bathroom fittings industry.

Emphasise On Brand Experience

A crucial aspect of brand positioning is delivering an exceptional brand experience to customers. Ensure that every touchpoint with your brand, from initial awareness to post-purchase support, reflects the values and promises of your brand positioning. Emphasizing the brand experience is crucial in the bathroom fittings industry as it helps create a lasting impression on customers and builds brand loyalty.

To emphasize the brand experience, it is essential to focus on every touchpoint where customers interact with your brand. Start by ensuring consistency across all brand elements, including visual identity, messaging, and tone of voice, to create a cohesive and memorable experience. Provide exceptional customer service by training your staff to be knowledgeable, helpful, and responsive to customer needs. Create engaging and user-friendly product displays and showroom experiences that allow customers to interact with your bathroom fittings and visualize them in their own spaces.

Leverage technology to enhance the brand experience, such as offering virtual reality tours or interactive online product configurators. Personalize the brand experience by understanding your customers' preferences and offering tailored recommendations or customization options. Encourage customer feedback and reviews, and use them as opportunities to improve and refine your brand experience.

Finally, go beyond the transactional aspect and create emotional connections with customers by telling your brand story, highlighting your values, and engaging in social and environmental initiatives. By emphasizing the brand experience, you can differentiate your brand from competitors, foster customer loyalty, and create a positive reputation in the bathroom fittings industry.

Let's read the story of a famous American brand called "AquaD"

They were known for their high-quality products and innovative designs. However, they realized that they needed to go beyond just offering great products to truly stand out in the competitive market. They decided to place a strong emphasis on brand experience.

AquaD understood that the bathroom is not just a functional space; it is a sanctuary where people relax and rejuvenate. They wanted their customers to have an exceptional experience from the moment they interacted with the brand. They revamped their showrooms to create a spa-like atmosphere, with soothing music, aromatic scents, and comfortable seating areas where customers could imagine their dream bathrooms.

But AquaD didn't stop there. They knew that the brand experience extended beyond the physical showroom. They invested in a user-friendly website where customers could explore their product range, visualize different bathroom setups, and even virtually experience their products through 3D simulations. They also provided comprehensive product information, including installation guides and maintenance tips, to ensure a seamless experience for their customers.

To further enhance the brand experience, AquaD implemented a customer-centric approach. Their well-trained staff members were not just knowledgeable about the products; they were also passionate about helping customers create their perfect bathroom spaces. They offered personalized consultations, taking the time to understand each customer's unique requirements and providing tailored recommendations.

AquaD also focused on post-purchase support. They established a dedicated customer service team that promptly addressed any queries or concerns. They even offered free installation assistance to ensure that customers had a hassle-free experience with their products.

As AquaD continued to prioritize brand experience, their customer satisfaction levels soared. Customers not only appreciated the quality and design of their products but also the overall experience of interacting with the brand. They shared their positive experiences through word-of-mouth, online reviews, and social media, becoming brand advocates for AquaD.

The emphasis on brand experience paid off for AquaD. Their customer base grew steadily, and they gained a reputation as a trusted and customer-centric brand in the bathroom fittings industry. They successfully differentiated themselves from their competitors by delivering an exceptional brand experience that went beyond the products themselves.

This story highlights the importance of emphasizing brand experience in the bathroom fittings industry. By creating a memorable and positive experience for customers at every touchpoint, AquaD was able to build a loyal customer base and establish themselves as a leader in the market. The story serves as a reminder that in a competitive industry, a strong brand experience can be a powerful differentiator and a key driver of success.

Build Emotional Connections

Building emotional connections with customers is a crucial aspect of brand building in the bathroom fittings industry. It goes beyond the functional aspects of the products and taps into the deeper desires and aspirations of the customers. When a brand can evoke positive emotions and create meaningful connections, it can cultivate strong customer loyalty and advocacy.

To build emotional connections, brands in the bathroom fittings industry need to understand their target audience on a deeper level. They must identify their customers' needs, desires, and values. By conducting thorough market research and customer surveys, brands can gain insights into what truly matters to their customers.

Once the emotional triggers are identified, brands can align their messaging and communication to resonate with their target audience. They can tell compelling stories that evoke emotions and create a sense of aspiration and inspiration. For example, a bathroom fittings brand can showcase how their products transform a mundane bathroom into a luxurious spa-like retreat, promoting a sense of relaxation and well-being.

Furthermore, brands can leverage various marketing channels to engage with customers and foster emotional connections. Social media platforms provide an excellent opportunity to showcase the brand's personality, share customer testimonials, and interact with customers directly. By responding to customer inquiries and feedback promptly and empathetically, brands can demonstrate their commitment to customer satisfaction and build trust.

In addition, brands can organize events or sponsor community initiatives that align with their brand values. This allows them to connect with customers on a more personal and emotional level, showing that they care about the same things their customers do. For example, a bathroom fittings brand can support environmental conservation efforts and promote sustainable practices, appealing to customers who value eco-friendly solutions.

Moreover, creating a seamless and delightful customer experience at every touchpoint is vital in building emotional connections. From the user-friendly website to the showroom ambiance and post-purchase support, every interaction should leave a positive and lasting impression. Personalized communication and attentive customer service further contribute to the emotional bond between the brand and its customers.

By building emotional connections, bathroom fittings brands can foster a sense of loyalty and advocacy among their customers. When customers feel emotionally connected to a brand, they become more than just buyers; they become brand advocates who willingly recommend the brand to others. This word-of-mouth marketing and positive reputation can significantly impact the brand's growth and success.

In conclusion, building emotional connections is a powerful strategy for bathroom fittings brands to differentiate themselves in the market and create lasting relationships with their customers. By understanding their target audience, crafting compelling stories, engaging through various channels, and providing exceptional customer experiences, brands can forge strong emotional bonds that go beyond the functional aspects of their products. These emotional connections not only drive customer loyalty but also foster brand advocacy, ultimately contributing to the long-term success and growth of the brand.

So, by strategically positioning your brand in the bathroom fittings market, you can differentiate yourself, attract your target audience, and build long-term success. Remember that effective brand positioning requires a deep understanding of your customers, market dynamics, and your brand's unique value proposition. Continuously refine your positioning strategies to stay relevant and meet the evolving needs of your customers.

CHAPTER 08

NURTURING CUSTOMER RELATIONSHIPS

The role of customer service and relationship management in building a strong brand

Nurturing customer relationships is a critical aspect with immense significance in building a strong brand in the bathroom fittings industry. The bathroom fittings market is highly competitive, and customers have a plethora of options to choose from. In such a scenario, establishing and maintaining strong customer relationships becomes crucial for brands to differentiate themselves and create a loyal customer base.

By focusing on customer relationships, brands can foster trust, loyalty, and advocacy, which are essential for long-term success. Building strong customer relationships allows brands to understand and meet customer needs effectively, provide personalized experiences, and exceed customer expectations. It enables brands to create positive customer experiences, which not only lead to repeat purchases but also generate positive word-of-mouth referrals.

Moreover, strong customer relationships contribute to brand reputation, as satisfied customers become brand advocates and ambassadors. They share their positive experiences with others, further enhancing the brand's visibility and credibility. In summary, nurturing customer relationships is a critical component for bathroom fittings brands to establish a strong brand presence, drive customer loyalty, and ultimately thrive in a competitive market.

Delivering Exceptional Customer Service

Delivering exceptional customer service is a cornerstone of building a strong brand in the bathroom fittings industry. It goes beyond simply selling products and encompasses the entire customer journey, from pre-sales inquiries to after-sales support. Exceptional customer service involves providing personalized attention, prompt responses, and going the extra mile to meet and exceed customer expectations.

One key aspect of delivering exceptional customer service is ensuring a seamless and hassle-free purchasing experience. Brands should strive to make the buying process as smooth as possible, offering clear product information, transparent pricing, and convenient payment options. This helps build trust and confidence in the brand, leaving a positive impression on customers.

Timely and effective communication is another crucial element of exceptional customer service. Responding promptly to customer inquiries, addressing concerns, and providing regular updates on order status are essential in fostering positive customer relationships. Brands should prioritize clear and open lines of communication through various channels, such as phone, email, live chat, and social media, to ensure customers feel supported and valued.

Furthermore, resolving customer issues and complaints in a proactive and satisfactory manner is vital for delivering exceptional customer service. Brands should have robust systems in place to handle customer feedback and complaints, promptly addressing any issues and taking appropriate actions to resolve them. This demonstrates the brand's commitment to customer satisfaction and helps build trust and loyalty.

Beyond the transactional aspects, exceptional customer service also involves building emotional connections with customers. Brands can achieve this by showing empathy, understanding customers' needs and preferences, and providing personalized recommendations or solutions. By treating customers as individuals and making them feel valued and appreciated, brands can create lasting emotional bonds and foster long-term loyalty.

Lastly, continuous improvement and feedback are essential for delivering exceptional customer service. Brands should actively seek feedback from customers, listen to their suggestions, and use the insights gained to enhance their products and services. By constantly striving to improve and innovate, brands can stay ahead of the competition and deliver exceptional experiences that keep customers coming back.

In summary, delivering exceptional customer service is a fundamental aspect of building a strong brand in the bathroom fittings industry. By prioritizing personalized attention, timely communication, issue resolution, emotional connections, and continuous improvement, brands can create positive customer experiences, foster loyalty, and differentiate themselves in a competitive market. Exceptional customer service not only leads to customer satisfaction and retention but also enhances the brand's reputation and attracts new customers through positive word-of-mouth.

Personalization and Tailored Solutions

Personalization and tailored solutions play a crucial role in nurturing customer relationships and building a strong brand in the bathroom fittings industry. In today's competitive market, customers expect brands to understand their unique needs and preferences and provide solutions that are specifically tailored to them.

Personalization goes beyond simply addressing customers by their names; it involves understanding their individual requirements and offering customized experiences. Brands can achieve personalization by collecting and analysing customer data, such as purchase history, preferences, and demographics. This data enables brands to segment their customer base and create targeted marketing campaigns and offers that resonate with specific customer groups.

One way to personalize the customer experience is by offering tailored product recommendations. By leveraging customer data and using advanced analytics, brands can suggest relevant products based on customers' past purchases, browsing behaviour, or expressed preferences. This not only enhances the shopping experience but also increases the chances of cross-selling and upselling, ultimately driving customer satisfaction and loyalty.

Another aspect of personalization is providing personalized customer support. Brands can leverage technology, such as chatbots or customer relationship management (CRM) systems, to track customer interactions and preferences. This allows customer service representatives to provide more personalized assistance, resolving queries and concerns in a timely and efficient manner. Additionally, brands can offer self-service options tailored to customer preferences, such as online product configurators or virtual design tools, allowing customers to personalize their own solutions.

Tailored solutions, on the other hand, involve going beyond standard product offerings and providing customized solutions to address specific customer needs. This can include working closely with customers to understand their requirements, collaborating with architects and interior designers for customized installations, or offering bespoke design services for unique projects. By offering tailored solutions, brands demonstrate their commitment to meeting customer expectations and providing added value.

Personalization and tailored solutions not only enhance the overall customer experience but also contribute to brand differentiation and customer loyalty. When customers feel that a brand understands and values their unique needs, they are more likely to develop a strong emotional connection and remain loyal over time. Moreover, personalized experiences lead to positive word-of-mouth recommendations, attracting new customers who seek similar levels of customization and tailored solutions.

In conclusion, personalization and tailored solutions are essential strategies for nurturing customer relationships and building a strong brand in the bathroom fittings industry. By leveraging customer data, offering personalized recommendations, providing customized customer support, and delivering tailored solutions, brands can create memorable experiences that resonate with customers on an individual level. This not only drives customer satisfaction and loyalty but also positions the brand as a trusted partner in meeting customers' specific needs.

Building Trust and Transparency

Building trust and transparency is a critical aspect of nurturing customer relationships and establishing a strong brand in the bathroom fittings industry. Trust is the foundation of any successful business relationship, and customers are more likely to engage with brands they perceive as trustworthy and transparent. When customers trust a brand, they feel confident in their purchasing decisions and are more likely to become loyal advocates.

To build trust, brands in the bathroom fittings industry should focus on several key elements. Firstly, it is essential to deliver on promises consistently. This means providing high-quality products that meet or exceed customer expectations, delivering products on time, and ensuring reliable after-sales service. By consistently delivering what is promised, brands demonstrate their commitment to customer satisfaction and build trust over time.

Transparency is another crucial aspect of building trust. Brands should be transparent about their manufacturing processes, sourcing of materials, and environmental practices. Sharing this information with customers not only establishes transparency but also allows customers to make informed choices based on their values. Brands can communicate their transparency through various channels, such as websites, product packaging, and marketing materials.

In addition to transparency, brands can also foster trust by being accessible and responsive to customer concerns. This includes providing multiple channels for customers to reach out, such as email, phone, or live chat, and ensuring timely and helpful responses. By actively listening to customer feedback and addressing any issues or concerns promptly, brands demonstrate their commitment to customer satisfaction and build trust through open and effective communication.

Another way to build trust is through social proof and testimonials. Displaying positive customer reviews, ratings, and testimonials on websites and social media platforms helps to establish credibility and build trust among potential customers. Additionally, brands can encourage satisfied customers to share their experiences and recommendations, further amplifying trust through word-of-mouth.

Furthermore, brands can build trust by prioritizing data security and privacy. With increasing concerns about data breaches and privacy violations, customers value brands that protect their personal information. Implementing robust data security measures, obtaining customer consent for data collection, and being transparent about data usage and protection can instil confidence and trust in customers.

Ultimately, building trust and transparency requires consistency, integrity, and a customer-centric approach. By focusing on delivering exceptional products and services, being transparent about business practices, actively listening and responding to customer feedback, and prioritizing data security, brands can foster trust and establish themselves as reliable partners in the bathroom fittings industry.

In conclusion, building trust and transparency is vital for nurturing customer relationships and building a strong brand in the bathroom fittings industry. By consistently delivering on promises, being transparent about business practices, being accessible and responsive to customer concerns, leveraging social proof, and prioritizing data security, brands can establish trust, enhance customer loyalty, and differentiate themselves in a competitive market. Trust and transparency not only contribute to customer satisfaction but also foster long-term brand success.

Proactive Communication and Engagement

Proactive communication and engagement play a crucial role in nurturing customer relationships and building a strong brand in the bathroom fittings industry. It involves taking the initiative to reach out to customers, anticipate their needs, and engage with them in a meaningful way. By proactively communicating and engaging with customers, brands can create positive experiences, build loyalty, and foster long-term relationships.

One aspect of proactive communication is keeping customers informed about new products, updates, and promotions. Brands can leverage various channels such as email newsletters, social media platforms, and blog posts to share relevant and valuable information with their customers. By providing regular updates, brands demonstrate their commitment to customer engagement and ensure that customers are aware of the latest offerings and developments.

In addition to sharing information, proactive communication involves actively seeking feedback and input from customers. Brands can use surveys, feedback forms, or even social media polls to gather insights and opinions from their customers. By inviting customers to share their thoughts, brands show that they value their input and are dedicated to continuous improvement. This two-way communication not only strengthens the relationship but also helps brands understand customer needs and preferences better.

Moreover, brands can proactively address customer concerns and issues before they escalate. This involves being attentive and responsive to customer inquiries, complaints, or suggestions. Brands should establish clear and efficient customer support channels, such as dedicated helplines or online chat systems, to ensure that customers can easily reach out for assistance. By promptly addressing customer concerns and providing satisfactory solutions, brands demonstrate their commitment to customer satisfaction and build trust.

Another aspect of proactive engagement is personalized communication. Brands can leverage customer data and insights to tailor their messages and offers to individual customers. By sending personalized recommendations, exclusive offers, or birthday greetings, brands make customers feel valued and appreciated. Personalization enhances the overall customer experience and strengthens the emotional connection between the brand and the customer.

Furthermore, proactive communication and engagement involve actively seeking opportunities to connect with customers beyond the point of sale. This can include sending follow-up emails after a purchase, conducting customer satisfaction surveys, or hosting customer appreciation events. By maintaining ongoing communication and engagement, brands can nurture long-term relationships and foster customer loyalty.

Lastly, brands can proactively engage with customers through social media platforms by responding to comments, sharing user-generated content, and participating in relevant conversations. By actively engaging with customers in these digital spaces, brands can strengthen their online presence, build a community of loyal followers, and amplify their brand message.

In conclusion, proactive communication and engagement are vital strategies for nurturing customer relationships and building a strong brand in the bathroom fittings industry. By proactively sharing information, seeking feedback, addressing concerns, personalizing communication, and engaging through various channels, brands can create positive experiences, build trust, and foster customer loyalty. Proactive communication and engagement demonstrate a brand's commitment to customer satisfaction and enhance the overall customer experience, contributing to long-term success in a competitive market.

Loyalty Programs and Rewards

Implementing customer loyalty programs and rewards is an effective strategy to cultivate long-term relationships. By offering exclusive benefits, discounts, and incentives, brands can incentivize repeat purchases and encourage customer loyalty. Loyalty programs also provide opportunities for brands to gather valuable customer data, which can be used to further personalize the customer experience and tailor marketing efforts. Here are some steps to create impactful loyalty programs and rewards:

Define your objectives: Clearly define the objectives of your loyalty program. Determine what you want to achieve, such as increasing customer retention, encouraging repeat purchases, or driving customer advocacy.

Segment your customer base: Segment your customer base based on factors like purchase history, frequency, and customer value. This allows you to tailor your loyalty program and rewards to specific customer segments, ensuring relevance and effectiveness.

Design appealing rewards: Develop a range of attractive rewards that incentivize customers to participate in your loyalty program. These rewards can include discounts on future purchases, exclusive access to new products, freebies, personalized offers, or points-based systems where customers can accumulate points and redeem them for rewards.

Make it easy to join and participate: Ensure that your loyalty program is easy to join and navigate. Simplify the sign-up process and provide clear instructions on how customers can earn and redeem rewards. Consider offering multiple ways for customers to earn rewards, such as making purchases, referring friends, or engaging with your brand on social media.

Personalize the experience: Tailor your loyalty program to individual customers by using customer data and preferences. Send personalized offers and rewards based on customer behaviour, preferences, and purchase history. This personalized approach enhances the customer experience and makes customers feel valued.

Communicate effectively: Regularly communicate with your loyalty program members to keep them engaged and informed about the program benefits, new rewards, and upcoming promotions. Utilize various communication channels, such as email, SMS, or a dedicated loyalty program portal, to stay connected with your customers.

Encourage engagement and referrals: Create opportunities for customers to engage with your brand and refer others to join your loyalty program. Offer additional rewards or bonuses for customer referrals, social media interactions, or participation in brand-related activities.

Monitor and analyse program performance: Continuously monitor the performance of your loyalty program by tracking key metrics such as customer retention, program engagement, and redemption rates. Analyse the data to identify trends, areas for improvement, and opportunities to optimize the program for better results.

Evolve and adapt: Regularly assess the effectiveness of your loyalty program and make necessary adjustments based on customer feedback and market trends. Stay updated with evolving customer expectations and preferences to ensure your loyalty program remains relevant and compelling.

Provide exceptional customer service: Deliver outstanding customer service to all loyalty program members. Address their queries or concerns promptly and provide a seamless experience throughout their engagement with your brand. Exceptional customer service reinforces the value of the loyalty program and enhances the overall customer experience.

By implementing these steps, you can create a compelling loyalty program that rewards and incentivizes customers, fostering loyalty and long-term relationships in the bathroom fittings industry. A well-designed loyalty program not only encourages repeat business but also helps create brand advocates who actively promote your products and services to others.

Continuous Improvement and Feedback

Continuous improvement and feedback play a vital role in nurturing customer relationships and building a strong brand in the bathroom fittings industry. It is essential to continuously evaluate and enhance your products, services, and customer interactions to meet evolving customer expectations and stay ahead of the competition. Here's how you can emphasize continuous improvement and feedback:

Firstly, actively seek feedback from your customers. Encourage them to share their experiences, suggestions, and concerns through various channels such as surveys, feedback forms, online reviews, or direct interactions. Pay attention to both positive and negative feedback, as they provide valuable insights into what is working well and areas that require improvement.

Secondly, analyse the feedback received and identify common themes or patterns. Look for recurring issues or suggestions that can guide your improvement efforts. This analysis will help you prioritize areas that need immediate attention and focus your resources effectively.

Next, use the feedback to drive innovation and product/service enhancements. Leverage customer insights to identify opportunities for new features, functionalities, or improvements in your bathroom fittings. Engage your product development and design teams to incorporate customer feedback into their processes, ensuring that your offerings align with customer needs and preferences.

Additionally, communicate with your customers about the actions taken based on their feedback. Let them know that their opinions are valued and demonstrate how their feedback has influenced your decisions and improvements. This builds trust and reinforces the notion that their voices are heard, fostering a sense of loyalty and engagement.

Furthermore, implement a culture of continuous improvement within your organization. Encourage employees at all levels to contribute ideas and suggestions for enhancing customer experience. Foster a learning environment where feedback is welcomed, and mistakes are seen as opportunities for growth and improvement.

Regularly review and evaluate your customer service processes and practices. Train your customer service representatives to actively listen to customer concerns, provide prompt resolutions, and handle feedback professionally. Encourage a customer-centric mindset throughout your organization, ensuring that every employee understands their role in delivering exceptional customer experiences.

Lastly, measure the impact of your improvement efforts and track key performance indicators to assess the effectiveness of your initiatives. Monitor customer satisfaction levels, customer retention rates, and other relevant metrics to gauge the success of your continuous improvement strategies. Use this data to make data-driven decisions and further refine your customer-centric approach.

By emphasizing continuous improvement and feedback, you demonstrate your commitment to delivering the best possible experiences to your customers. This iterative process allows you to stay agile, adapt to changing customer needs, and consistently enhance your brand's value proposition. Ultimately, it leads to increased customer satisfaction, loyalty, and advocacy, strengthening your brand's position in the bathroom fittings industry.

Resolving Customer Complaints

Resolving customer complaints effectively is a critical aspect of nurturing customer relationships and building a strong brand in the bathroom fittings industry. Customer complaints provide an opportunity to turn a negative experience into a positive one, showcase your commitment to customer satisfaction, and build trust and loyalty. Here's how you can effectively resolve customer complaints:

Promptly acknowledge and listen: When a customer raises a complaint, acknowledge it promptly and show empathy. Listen carefully to their concerns without interruption, allowing them to express their frustrations or disappointments fully. Make the customer feel heard and understood, as this can help de-escalate the situation and create a foundation for resolution.

Investigate and gather information: Thoroughly investigate the complaint by gathering all relevant information. This may involve reviewing purchase records, examining product specifications, or consulting with relevant departments. Ensure that you have a clear understanding of the issue before proceeding with a resolution.

Provide a swift and appropriate solution: Once you have identified the root cause of the complaint, offer a solution that is fair, reasonable, and tailored to the customer's specific situation. This may involve providing a replacement product, offering a refund or discount, scheduling a repair or service, or taking any other necessary steps to address the customer's concerns.

Communicate effectively: Clearly communicate the proposed solution to the customer, explaining the steps you will take to resolve their complaint. Be transparent about any limitations or constraints that may exist and manage their expectations accordingly. Maintain open lines of communication throughout the process, keeping the customer informed of progress and any updates.

Take ownership and responsibility: Take full ownership of the complaint and the resolution process. Ensure that the customer feels that their concerns are being taken seriously and that you are committed to resolving the issue to their satisfaction. Avoid shifting blame or making excuses, as this can further frustrate the customer and damage your brand reputation.

Follow up and ensure satisfaction: After implementing the solution, follow up with the customer to ensure their satisfaction. Confirm that the complaint has been resolved to their expectations and address any remaining concerns. This demonstrates your commitment to customer service and reinforces the positive perception of your brand.

Learn from complaints: View customer complaints as learning opportunities. Analyse the root causes of recurring complaints and identify areas for improvement in your products, services, or processes. Use this feedback to make necessary changes and prevent similar issues from arising in the future.

Train and empower your customer service team: Provide comprehensive training to your customer service representatives to equip them with the skills and knowledge necessary to handle customer complaints effectively. Empower them to make decisions within defined guidelines, enabling them to resolve issues promptly and efficiently.

By effectively resolving customer complaints, you not only address individual customer concerns but also demonstrate your commitment to customer satisfaction and continuous improvement. Customers who experience a satisfactory resolution to their complaints are more likely to remain loyal and become brand advocates, positively impacting your brand's reputation and growth in the bathroom fittings industry.

To summarise, in the bathroom fittings industry, nurturing customer relationships through exceptional customer service and relationship management is key to building a strong brand. By delivering exceptional service, personalizing experiences, building trust, engaging proactively, implementing loyalty programs, continuously improving based on feedback, and resolving complaints effectively, brands can create loyal and satisfied customers who become advocates for the brand. These customer relationships contribute to the long-term success and growth of the brand by fostering customer loyalty, driving repeat business, and generating positive word-of-mouth recommendations.

CHAPTER 09

LEVERAGING DIGITAL MARKETING FOR BRAND GROWTH

How to use digital channels, including social media and SEO, to grow your brand?

In today's digital age, leveraging digital marketing strategies is crucial for brand growth in the bathroom fittings industry. Digital channels provide immense opportunities to connect with a wider audience, increase brand visibility, and drive customer engagement. This chapter explores various aspects of digital marketing and how you can effectively use digital channels to grow your brand. Here are key insights and strategies to leverage digital marketing for brand growth:

Harness the power of social media

Social media platforms offer a vast reach and allow you to engage with your target audience directly. Create a strong presence on popular social media platforms such as Facebook, Instagram, Twitter, and LinkedIn. Develop a content strategy that aligns with your brand's values and objectives, and consistently share engaging and informative content to build a loyal following. Encourage user-generated content and actively respond to comments, messages, and reviews to foster meaningful connections with your audience. Here are some key steps to effectively utilize social media for your brand:

Set clear goals: Define your objectives for social media marketing. Determine whether you want to increase brand awareness, drive website traffic, generate leads, foster customer engagement, or promote specific products or campaigns. Setting clear goals will guide your social media strategy and help you measure success.

Identify the right platforms: Research and understand which social media platforms are most relevant to your target audience. Consider factors such as demographics, user behaviour, and industry trends. Focus your efforts on platforms where your audience is most active to maximize your reach and engagement.

Develop a content strategy: Create a content plan that aligns with your brand identity and objectives. Define the types of content you will share, such as informative articles, engaging videos, eye-catching images, or user-generated content. Maintain a consistent posting schedule to keep your audience engaged and build anticipation.

Engage with your audience: Social media is a two-way communication channel. Encourage interactions by responding to comments, messages, and mentions in a timely manner. Show appreciation for positive feedback and address concerns or inquiries promptly. Engaging with your audience humanizes your brand and fosters strong connections.

Leverage visual elements: Visual content is highly engaging on social media. Use high-quality images, videos, infographics, and other visual elements to capture attention and convey your brand's message effectively. Invest in professional photography or graphic design if needed to maintain a visually appealing and cohesive brand presence.

Utilize storytelling techniques: Tell compelling stories that resonate with your audience. Share behind-the-scenes glimpses, customer success stories, or narratives that showcase your brand's values and mission. Storytelling creates an emotional connection and helps differentiate your brand from competitors.

Use hashtags strategically: Hashtags help categorize your content and make it discoverable to a wider audience. Research relevant and trending hashtags in the bathroom fittings industry and incorporate them into your posts. Develop branded hashtags to encourage user-generated content and facilitate brand recognition.

Collaborate with influencers: Influencers have established credibility and a loyal following on social media. Partnering with influencers who align with your brand can expand your reach and attract new followers. Collaborate on sponsored content, product reviews, or influencer takeovers to leverage their influence and increase brand visibility.

Stay updated with trends and algorithms: Social media platforms continuously evolve their algorithms and introduce new features. Stay informed about the latest trends, updates, and best practices. Adapt your strategy accordingly to leverage new features and stay relevant in the ever-changing social media landscape.

By following these steps, you can harness the power of social media to build brand awareness, engage your target audience, and drive growth in the bathroom fittings industry. Remember to be authentic, consistent, and responsive in your social media interactions to create a positive brand image and establish long-lasting connections with your followers.

Optimize your website for search engines

Implement search engine optimization (SEO) techniques to improve your website's visibility in search engine results. Conduct keyword research relevant to the bathroom fittings industry and incorporate them naturally into your website content, meta tags, and headings. Create informative and valuable content that addresses the needs and interests of your target audience. Optimize your website's load speed, mobile responsiveness, and user experience to enhance engagement and drive organic traffic. Here are some key strategies to optimize your website for search engines:

Keyword research: Identify relevant keywords and phrases that your target audience is likely to use when searching for bathroom fittings. Use keyword research tools to discover high-volume and low-competition keywords. Incorporate these keywords strategically into your website content, including page titles, headings, meta descriptions, and body text.

On-page optimization: Ensure that each page of your website is properly optimized. Optimize the URL structure, include descriptive meta tags, and use header tags (H1, H2, H3) to structure your content. Make sure your content is informative, well-structured, and easy to read. Include relevant keywords naturally within the content, but avoid keyword stuffing.

High-quality content: Create valuable and relevant content that meets the needs of your target audience. Publish blog posts, articles, guides, and other informative content related to bathroom fittings. Use your expertise to provide insights, tips, and solutions. Engaging and informative content helps attract visitors, keeps them on your website longer, and encourages them to share your content.

Mobile optimization: With the increasing use of mobile devices, optimizing your website for mobile is crucial. Ensure that your website is responsive and mobile-friendly, adapting to different screen sizes and resolutions. Optimize page load speed to provide a seamless browsing experience on mobile devices.

User experience: User experience plays a significant role in search engine optimization. Ensure that your website is easy to navigate, with clear menu structures and internal linking. Improve page load speed by optimizing image sizes, using caching mechanisms, and minimizing code. Make sure your website is visually appealing, with a clean and professional design.

Link building: Build high-quality backlinks to your website from reputable and relevant sources. Seek opportunities for guest blogging, collaborations, and partnerships with industry influencers or related websites. Backlinks from authoritative websites can improve your website's credibility and visibility in search engine rankings.

Technical optimization: Pay attention to technical aspects of your website's optimization. Ensure proper indexing by search engines through the use of XML sitemaps and robots.txt files. Optimize your website's load speed, eliminate duplicate content, and fix broken links. Regularly monitor and resolve any technical issues that may affect your website's performance.

Local SEO: If you have a physical store or serve a specific geographic area, optimize your website for local search. Claim your business listing on Google My Business, include your address, contact information, and operating hours. Optimize your website content with location-specific keywords and create location pages if applicable.

Analytics and monitoring: Implement web analytics tools such as Google Analytics to track and measure the performance of your website. Monitor key metrics such as organic traffic, bounce rate, time on site, and conversion rates. Use these insights to identify areas for improvement and refine your SEO strategies.

You can optimize your website for search engines and improve your visibility in the bathroom fittings industry. But, remember that search engine optimization is an ongoing process, and it's essential to stay updated with industry trends and algorithm changes to maintain your website's optimization and ranking.

Invest In Paid Online Advertising

Consider allocating a portion of your marketing budget to paid online advertising channels such as Google Ads, social media ads, and display advertising. These platforms offer precise targeting options, allowing you to reach your desired audience effectively. Here is a step-by-step guide for you on paid online advertising:

- Craft compelling ad copies and visuals that highlight your unique selling points and drive click-through rates

- Monitor the performance of your ads and optimize them based on analytics to maximize their effectiveness
- Determine the objectives of your advertising campaign, whether it's increasing brand awareness, driving website traffic, generating leads, or boosting sales
- Clearly define your target audience to ensure your ads reach the right people
- **Choose the right platforms:** Identify the digital platforms where your target audience is most active. Consider popular advertising platforms such as Google Ads, social media platforms like Facebook, Instagram, and LinkedIn, and industry-specific websites or forums
- Choose the appropriate ad formats based on your goals and target audience. Options may include display ads, search ads, video ads, native ads, or sponsored content. Each format has its own strengths and can be tailored to specific campaign objectives
- Determine your advertising budget and allocate it strategically across different platforms and campaigns. Test different budget allocations and monitor the performance of each campaign to optimize your spending
- Create engaging and visually appealing ad creatives that capture attention and effectively communicate your brand's message. Use persuasive copy, compelling visuals, and clear calls-to-action to entice users to click on your ads
- Refine your targeting options to reach the most relevant audience. Utilize demographic targeting, geographic

targeting, interests, behaviour, and retargeting options to optimize your ad delivery

- Continuously monitor the performance of your paid advertising campaigns. Track key metrics such as impressions, clicks, click-through rates, conversion rates, and return on ad spend. Adjust your campaigns based on the data and insights you gather to optimize performance

- Conduct A/B testing by creating variations of your ad creatives, headlines, and calls-to-action. Test different versions to identify the most effective elements and optimize your ads accordingly

- Lastly, implement conversion tracking tools to measure the effectiveness of your ads in generating desired actions, such as form submissions, purchases, or newsletter sign-ups. This data will help you evaluate the return on your advertising investment

- Regularly analyse the results of your paid advertising campaigns and make data-driven decisions to improve performance

Experiment with different targeting options, ad formats, and messaging to optimize your ads for better results. Investing in paid online advertising can significantly enhance your brand's visibility, drive targeted traffic, and generate valuable leads in the bathroom fittings industry. By strategically planning and executing your advertising campaigns, you can maximize the impact of your investment and achieve your marketing objectives.

Implement email marketing campaigns

Email marketing remains a powerful tool for nurturing

customer relationships and driving repeat business. Build an email subscriber list by offering valuable content, exclusive promotions, or industry insights in exchange for email addresses. Segment your subscribers based on their preferences and behaviours, and tailor your email campaigns accordingly. Personalize your emails, provide relevant product recommendations, and leverage automation to send timely and targeted messages. Here are some steps to make your email marketing campaigns effective:

Build a targeted email list: Create a database of customers, prospects, and leads who have opted in to receive emails from your brand. Segment your list based on factors such as demographics, purchase history, and interests to send relevant and personalized emails.

Define campaign goals: Clearly define the goals of your email marketing campaigns. Whether it's promoting new products, driving website traffic, or nurturing customer relationships, having specific goals will help you tailor your content and measure the success of your campaigns.

Craft compelling subject lines: The subject line is the first thing your recipients see, so make it enticing and compelling. Grab their attention and make them curious to open your emails. Use personalized subject lines, offers, or intriguing statements to pique their interest.

Create engaging content: Provide valuable and engaging content in your emails. Share industry insights, product updates, helpful tips, or exclusive offers. Use a mix of text, images, and videos to make your emails visually appealing and easy to consume.

Personalize your emails: Personalization goes beyond just addressing recipients by name. Use customer data to personalize the content of your emails. Segment your audience based on their preferences, purchase history, or location, and tailor your messages accordingly.

Design mobile-friendly emails: Ensure your emails are optimized for mobile devices. With a large portion of email opens happening on mobile, it's crucial to have responsive designs that adapt to different screen sizes. Test your emails on various devices and email clients to ensure a seamless experience.

Include clear calls-to-action (CTAs): Every email should have a clear purpose and a call-to-action. Whether it's directing recipients to your website, inviting them to a webinar, or encouraging them to make a purchase, use persuasive CTAs that stand out and drive action.

Test and optimize: Continuously test different elements of your email campaigns, such as subject lines, content, CTAs, and send times. A/B testing allows you to compare different versions of your emails and determine what resonates best with your audience. Use the insights gained from testing to optimize your campaigns for better results.

Monitor and analyse metrics: Track key email marketing metrics like open rates, click-through rates, conversion rates, and unsubscribe rates. Monitor the performance of your campaigns and analyse the data to gain insights into what works and what needs improvement. Use this data to refine your email marketing strategy.

Maintain compliance: Ensure that your email marketing campaigns comply with applicable laws and regulations, such as obtaining consent from recipients and providing easy unsubscribe options. Stay updated on email marketing best practices and industry guidelines to maintain a positive reputation and deliverability.

By implementing effective email marketing campaigns, you can nurture relationships with your audience, drive engagement, and achieve your marketing objectives in the bathroom fittings industry. Remember to deliver valuable content, personalize your messages, and continuously optimize your campaigns for better results.

Foster online reviews and testimonials

Positive reviews and testimonials act as social proof and influence the purchasing decisions of potential customers. Encourage satisfied customers to leave reviews on platforms such as Google My Business, Yelp, and industry-specific websites. Respond to reviews, both positive and negative, in a professional and timely manner to show that you value customer feedback. Showcase testimonials on your website and social media platforms to build trust and credibility.

Getting online reviews and testimonials is a crucial aspect of building trust and credibility for your brand in the bathroom fittings industry. Positive reviews and testimonials from satisfied customers can influence potential buyers and help them make informed purchasing decisions. Here are some strategies to encourage and collect online reviews and testimonials:

1. Make it easy for customers to leave reviews by providing clear instructions and user-friendly platforms

2. Consider utilizing popular review sites or integrating a review feature on your website

3. Reach out to your customers and request their feedback after their purchase or experience with your bathroom fittings
4. Send personalized emails or messages asking for their honest opinion about their satisfaction level and encourage them to share their experience online

Also, try to Incentivize customers to leave reviews by offering small rewards or discounts. This can motivate them to take the time to share their feedback and increase the likelihood of receiving positive reviews. Engage with your customers on social media platforms and encourage them to leave reviews or testimonials. Share positive reviews on your social media channels to showcase customer satisfaction and encourage others to share their experiences.

You can display testimonials prominently on your website to highlight the positive experiences of your customers. Include their names, photos (with their permission), and any relevant details that add credibility to their testimonials. Show that you value customer feedback by responding to both positive and negative reviews. Acknowledge positive reviews with gratitude and address any concerns raised in negative reviews promptly and professionally. This demonstrates your commitment to customer satisfaction.

By consistently delivering outstanding customer service, you increase the chances of receiving positive reviews and testimonials. When customers have a positive experience with your brand, they are more likely to share their satisfaction with others. Regularly monitor online review platforms and social media channels to stay informed about what customers are saying about your brand. Respond to reviews promptly and address any issues raised. This proactive approach shows that you value customer feedback and are committed to continuous improvement.

Remember, genuine and authentic reviews are essential for building trust. Encourage customers to share their honest opinions and experiences, and always respond graciously to feedback. Utilize the power of positive reviews and testimonials to enhance your brand's online reputation and attract more customers in the bathroom fittings industry.

Embrace video marketing

Video content has gained immense popularity and engagement in the digital landscape. Create engaging and informative videos that highlight your brand, products, and customer stories. Share video content on platforms like YouTube, Instagram, and Facebook to attract and engage your target audience. Consider live streaming events, tutorials, and behind-the-scenes footage to add a personal touch and foster a stronger connection with your audience. Effective video marketing can be a powerful tool to engage and connect with your target audience in the bathroom fittings industry. Here are some key strategies to create impactful video content:

1. **Clearly define the goals and objectives of your video marketing campaign**

   Are you looking to increase brand awareness, showcase product features, or educate your audience? Identifying your objectives will help guide your video creation process. Next you need to understand your target audience's preferences, interests, and pain points. This knowledge will enable you to create video content that resonates with them and addresses their specific needs.

2. **Develop a content strategy that aligns with your brand message and objectives**

   Plan your videos based on different stages of the customer journey, such as awareness, consideration, and decision-making. This will ensure that your videos effectively guide viewers through the buyer's journey.

3. **Storytelling is a powerful technique in video marketing**

   Craft narratives that captivate your audience and evoke emotions. Whether it's showcasing a customer's success story, highlighting the craftsmanship of your bathroom fittings, or sharing behind-the-scenes glimpses, stories help create a memorable connection with your brand.

   Attention spans are short, so aim for concise and engaging videos. Capture your audience's attention within the first few seconds and maintain their interest throughout the video. Use visuals, animations, music, and compelling narration to create an immersive experience.

4. **Demonstrate the features, benefits, and unique selling points of your bathroom fittings in a visually appealing way**

   Highlight the quality, durability, and innovative aspects of your products through close-ups, demonstrations, and customer testimonials. Tailor your videos for different social media platforms and online channels. Optimize video lengths, formats, and styles to suit each platform's requirements and best practices. Consider creating teaser videos, tutorials, product showcases, or even live-streaming events to engage your audience effectively.

5. **Do not forget to include clear and compelling CTAs in your videos**

   Direct viewers to visit your website, subscribe to your channel, follow you on social media, or take any other desired action. CTAs help drive engagement, conversions, and brand interaction.

6. **Maintain consistency in your video content to reinforce your brand identity**

   Be authentic, transparent, and true to your brand values. Building trust and credibility through genuine video content will help establish long-term connections with your audience.

By implementing these strategies, you can create effective video marketing campaigns that resonate with your target audience, increase brand awareness, and drive engagement in the bathroom fittings industry.

Monitor and analyse your digital marketing efforts

Regularly monitor key performance indicators (KPIs) such as website traffic, engagement metrics, conversion rates, and social media insights. Leverage analytics tools to gain insights into the effectiveness of your digital marketing campaigns. Use this data to refine your strategies, identify areas for improvement, and capitalize on opportunities for growth.

By effectively leveraging digital marketing strategies, you can expand your brand's reach, increase customer engagement, and drive growth in the competitive bathroom fittings industry. Embrace the power of social media, optimize your website for search engines, invest in paid advertising, implement email marketing campaigns, create valuable content, encourage online reviews, embrace video marketing, and monitor your efforts to achieve optimal results. Stay updated with the latest digital marketing trends and adapt your strategies accordingly to stay ahead in the digital landscape.

CHAPTER 10

EVALUATING BRAND SUCCESS

Tools and metrics for measuring the success of your branding efforts and making necessary adjustments

Measuring the success of your branding efforts is crucial to ensure that your strategies are effective and delivering the desired results. In this last Chapter, we look into the tools and metrics you can use to evaluate the success of your brand and make necessary adjustments. Here are some key aspects to consider when evaluating brand success:

Brand Awareness

When it comes to evaluating brand success, measuring brand awareness is a critical aspect. Brand awareness refers to the level of familiarity and recognition your brand has among your target audience. It indicates how well your brand is known and remembered by consumers. Measure the level of awareness and recognition your brand has achieved among your target audience. This can be assessed through surveys, brand recall studies, and social media analytics to gauge the reach and visibility of your brand. Here are some key methods to assess and measure brand awareness:

Surveys: Conducting surveys can provide valuable insights into brand awareness. You can design surveys that include questions related to brand recognition, recall, and overall awareness. By asking respondents about their familiarity with your brand, you can gauge the extent to which your brand is known within your target market.

Brand Recall Studies: Brand recall studies involve assessing the ability of consumers to remember your brand when prompted with specific cues or stimuli. These studies help determine if your brand is top-of-mind for consumers in relevant contexts. By measuring brand recall, you can gain insights into the effectiveness of your brand's marketing efforts and its impact on consumer memory.

Social Media Analytics: Social media platforms provide a wealth of data that can be utilized to measure brand awareness. By analysing metrics such as reach, impressions, engagement, and follower growth, you can assess the visibility and reach of your brand on social media. Monitoring brand mentions, hashtags, and user-generated content can also give you an idea of how actively your brand is being discussed and shared among social media users.

Website Traffic: Monitoring website traffic can serve as an indicator of brand awareness. By analysing the number of visitors to your website, the sources of traffic, and the time spent on your site, you can determine the level of interest and engagement with your brand. Increased website traffic suggests a higher level of brand awareness and indicates that consumers are actively seeking out information about your brand.

Online Search Volume: Monitoring online search volume for your brand name and related keywords can provide insights into brand awareness. Higher search volume indicates that consumers are actively searching for your brand, products, or services, which signifies a strong level of brand recognition.

Brand Mentions and PR Coverage: Keeping track of brand mentions in media outlets, publications, and online platforms can give you an indication of your brand's visibility and awareness in the public domain. Positive media coverage and mentions contribute to building brand awareness and credibility.

By utilizing a combination of these methods, you can gain a comprehensive understanding of your brand's awareness levels among your target audience. This data will help you identify areas of strength and areas that require improvement. By consistently monitoring brand awareness metrics, you can track the progress of your branding efforts and make informed decisions to enhance brand recognition and visibility.

Customer Perception

Assessing customer perception is a crucial aspect of evaluating brand success. Customer perception refers to how customers perceive and interpret your brand, including their opinions, attitudes, and beliefs about your products, services, and overall brand experience. Here are some key methods to check customer perception:

Conducting surveys and gathering customer feedback is an effective way to gauge customer perception. You can ask customers to rate their satisfaction levels, provide feedback on their experiences with your brand, and assess their perceptions of your brand attributes. By collecting and analysing this data, you can gain insights into how customers perceive your brand and identify areas for improvement.

Monitoring online reviews and ratings on platforms such as review websites, social media, and e-commerce platforms can provide valuable insights into customer perception. Positive reviews and high ratings indicate that customers have a favourable perception of your brand, while negative reviews can highlight areas that need attention.

Engaging in social media listening involves monitoring conversations and mentions of your brand on social media platforms. By analysing what customers are saying about your brand, their sentiments, and the topics they discuss, you can gain a deeper understanding of customer perception. This information can help you identify strengths, weaknesses, and areas where you can make improvements.

Conducting in-depth interviews and focus groups with customers can provide qualitative insights into their perceptions. These discussions allow you to dig deeper into their experiences, preferences, and opinions about your brand. By listening to their stories and perspectives, you can uncover valuable insights that help shape your brand strategy.

Assessing your brand's reputation through reputation management tools and analysis can give you a sense of how customers perceive your brand in the larger market. Monitoring brand sentiment, media coverage, and public opinion can help you gauge the overall perception of your brand among customers and stakeholders.

By actively checking customer perception through these methods, you can gain valuable insights into how your brand is perceived in the market. This information will enable you to make informed decisions to improve customer satisfaction, enhance brand reputation, and align your brand image with the desired perception among your target audience. Regularly assessing customer perception allows you to make necessary adjustments and maintain a positive brand image in the eyes of your customers.

Sales Performance

Analyse sales data to understand the impact of your branding efforts on revenue generation

Analysing sales performance is crucial for understanding the impact of your branding efforts on revenue generation and overall business success. By tracking key performance indicators (KPIs) related to sales, you can assess the effectiveness of your branding strategies and determine the direct influence of your brand on business outcomes. Track key performance indicators such as sales growth, customer acquisition rates, and repeat purchases to determine the direct influence of your brand on business outcomes. Here are some key areas to focus on when evaluating sales performance:

Sales Growth: Monitor your sales growth over time to assess the overall performance of your brand. Track revenue growth percentages and compare them against previous periods or industry benchmarks. A positive sales growth indicates that your branding efforts are resonating with customers and driving increased sales.

Customer Acquisition Rates: Measure how effectively your branding efforts are attracting new customers. Monitor the number of new customers acquired within a specific period and analyse the sources or marketing channels that contribute to customer acquisition. This data helps you identify which branding initiatives are most successful in bringing in new business.

Repeat Purchases and Customer Retention: Evaluate the rate of repeat purchases from existing customers to gauge their satisfaction and loyalty. A high rate of repeat purchases indicates that your branding has successfully created a positive customer experience, leading to customer loyalty and retention. Additionally, track customer churn rates to identify areas where improvements can be made to enhance customer retention.

Average Order Value: Assess the average value of each customer's purchase to understand the effectiveness of your branding in influencing buying behaviour. A higher average order value suggests that your branding has successfully communicated value and positioned your brand as a premium choice in the market. Analyse whether specific branding initiatives or promotions are driving higher-value purchases.

Sales Conversion Rates: Monitor the conversion rates at various stages of the sales funnel, from lead to sale. This helps you identify potential bottlenecks in the customer journey and optimize your branding and sales strategies accordingly. Analyse conversion rates at each touchpoint to pinpoint areas for improvement and enhance the effectiveness of your brand messaging and customer engagement.

Sales by Product or Service Category: Evaluate the performance of different product or service categories within your brand portfolio. Identify which offerings are driving the majority of sales and assess whether they align with your brand positioning and target market. This analysis can guide product development decisions and help you focus your branding efforts on high-performing areas.

Brand Impact on Sales: Analyse the correlation between your branding efforts and sales performance. Look for patterns or trends that indicate a direct impact of your brand on driving sales. This can include analysing the sales performance of specific marketing campaigns, promotions, or branding initiatives. Determine the ROI of your branding investments by quantifying the incremental sales attributed to these activities.

Customer Feedback and Surveys: Collect customer feedback and conduct surveys to gather insights into their perception of your brand and its impact on their purchasing decisions. Ask customers about their experience with your brand, their satisfaction levels, and their likelihood to recommend your brand to others. This qualitative data provides valuable insights into the effectiveness of your branding efforts in influencing customer behaviour.

Competitive Analysis: Compare your sales performance to that of your competitors to assess your brand's market position. Analyse market share, sales growth rates, and customer preferences to understand how your brand is performing relative to others in the industry. This analysis helps identify areas where you can differentiate your brand and capitalize on opportunities for growth.

Continuous Improvement: Regularly review and analyse sales performance data to identify areas for improvement and inform future branding strategies. Use the insights gained to refine your branding initiatives, optimize your marketing campaigns, and enhance customer engagement. Embrace a culture of continuous improvement, leveraging data-driven insights to drive ongoing success.

By analysing sales data and key performance indicators, you can gain valuable insights into the impact of your branding efforts on revenue generation and customer behaviour. This information allows you to make data-driven decisions, refine your branding strategies, and optimize your sales approach to drive sustainable brand growth.

Market Share

Assess your brand's market share and compare it to your competitors. This will provide insights into your brand's position within the industry and its ability to capture a significant portion of the market. Evaluating your brand's market share is an essential aspect of measuring its success and competitiveness in the industry. Here are key considerations for evaluating market share:

Start by **defining the market** in which your brand operates. Consider factors such as geography, product category, and target audience. This ensures that you have a clear understanding of the market in which you want to assess your brand's share.

Determine the total market size by evaluating industry reports, market research data, or internal sales data. This provides an estimate of the overall size of the market and serves as a benchmark for measuring your brand's share.

Also, calculate your **brand's total sales or revenue** within the defined market. This can be obtained from your financial records or sales reports. Ensure that the sales data is specific to the market you are analysing.

Research and gather information on your competitors' sales or revenue within the same market. This can be obtained from public reports, industry data, or competitor analysis.

Calculate their market share by dividing their sales by the total market size. Divide your brand's sales by the total market size and multiply by 100 to obtain your brand's market share percentage. This indicates the proportion of the market that your brand currently captures.

Then **compare** your brand's market share with that of your competitors to assess your brand's relative position in the market. Identify competitors who have a higher market share and analyse their strategies to understand their success factors. Take into account the growth rate of the overall market when evaluating your market share. If your brand's market share remains constant while the market is expanding, it may indicate a loss of market share in relative terms.

Analyse the factors that contribute to your brand's market share. Consider aspects such as brand recognition, customer loyalty, pricing strategies, product differentiation, distribution channels, and marketing efforts.

Identify areas where you can **leverage your strengths or improve weaknesses** to increase your market share. Continuously monitor and track your brand's market share over time to identify trends and changes in the competitive landscape. This helps you evaluate the effectiveness of your branding and marketing strategies and make necessary adjustments.

If your brand's market share is lower than desired, develop strategies to increase your market presence. This may involve enhancing your brand's value proposition, expanding your product offerings, targeting new customer segments, improving customer experience, or implementing aggressive marketing campaigns.

Evaluating market share provides valuable insights into your brand's competitiveness and market position. It helps you understand how well your brand is performing in relation to competitors and guides strategic decision-making. By monitoring and taking action to increase your market share, you can strengthen your brand's presence, attract more customers, and drive sustainable growth in the bathroom fittings industry.

Return on Investment (ROI)

Evaluating the return on investment (ROI) of marketing expenses is crucial to determine the effectiveness and profitability of your marketing efforts. It allows you to measure the financial impact of your marketing activities and make informed decisions about resource allocation. Here's how you can evaluate the ROI of marketing expenses:

Define Goals and Objectives: Start by establishing clear goals and objectives for your marketing campaigns. These could include increasing brand awareness, driving website traffic, generating leads, boosting sales, or improving customer retention. Setting specific, measurable, achievable, relevant, and time-bound (SMART) goals helps align your marketing efforts with desired outcomes.

Track Marketing Expenses: Keep a detailed record of all marketing expenses incurred, including advertising costs, campaign creation and management fees, content creation, marketing software subscriptions, design and production costs, and any other marketing-related investments.

Measure Key Performance Indicators (KPIs): Identify the key performance indicators (KPIs) that align with your marketing objectives. These could include website traffic, conversions, sales revenue, customer acquisition cost (CAC), customer lifetime value (CLV), lead generation, email open rates, social media engagement, or any other metrics relevant to your business goals.

Assign Monetary Values: Assign monetary values to the outcomes associated with your marketing activities. For example, calculate the revenue generated from each marketing campaign or the average lifetime value of a customer acquired through marketing efforts. This allows you to attribute financial gains or losses to specific marketing initiatives.

Calculate ROI: To calculate the ROI of your marketing expenses, use the following formula:

ROI = (Net Profit - Marketing Expenses) / Marketing Expenses * 100

Net Profit is the revenue generated or cost savings achieved as a result of your marketing efforts. Deduct the total marketing expenses from the net profit to obtain the net gain attributable to marketing. Divide this net gain by the marketing expenses and multiply by 100 to express the ROI as a percentage.

Analyse and Compare Results: Analyse the ROI for each marketing campaign or initiative separately to assess their individual performance. Compare the ROI across different marketing channels, campaigns, or time periods to identify the most effective and efficient strategies. This analysis helps you allocate resources to the most impactful marketing activities.

Consider the Customer Lifetime Value (CLV): When evaluating ROI, take into account the CLV of acquired customers. Some marketing initiatives may have a lower ROI in the short term but contribute significantly to long-term customer retention and value. Understanding the CLV allows you to prioritize investments that yield sustainable profitability.

Monitor and Refine: Continuously monitor and track the performance of your marketing campaigns and adjust your strategies accordingly. Regularly review and update your marketing goals, KPIs, and ROI calculations to ensure they remain aligned with your business objectives.

Benchmark and Industry Comparison: Compare your marketing ROI with industry benchmarks or competitors' performance to gain insights into your brand's relative effectiveness. This comparison helps identify areas of improvement and competitive advantages.

Optimize and Improve: Use the insights gained from evaluating the ROI of marketing expenses to optimize your marketing strategies. Allocate resources to initiatives with higher ROI, refine targeting and messaging, experiment with new tactics, and continuously seek opportunities to improve the efficiency and effectiveness of your marketing efforts.

To conclude, by utilising these tools and metrics, you can effectively evaluate the success of your branding efforts and make data-driven decisions to optimize your brand performance. Regular evaluation and adjustments are essential to ensure that your brand remains relevant, resonates with your target audience, and drives business growth.

CONCLUSION

This book titled **"The Branding Blueprint: Become A Leader in Bathroom Fittings Industry"** is a comprehensive guide that equips readers with the knowledge and strategies to build a strong and successful brand in the competitive bathroom fittings market. Throughout the book, we have explored the critical aspects of branding, from understanding the industry landscape to crafting a unique brand identity, positioning the brand effectively, nurturing customer relationships, leveraging digital marketing, and evaluating brand success.

Branding plays a pivotal role in establishing a distinct identity and gaining a competitive edge in the bathroom fittings industry. By effectively implementing the strategies and insights shared in this book, businesses can create a brand that resonates with their target audience, differentiates them from competitors, and builds long-lasting customer relationships.

Furthermore, we have emphasized the significance of understanding the target audience, conducting market research, and developing a strong value proposition. By aligning the brand's messaging, visual identity, and customer experience, businesses can create a cohesive and compelling brand that captures the attention and loyalty of customers.

In today's digital era, leveraging digital marketing channels and embracing technology is essential for brand growth. The book has explored the power of social media, search engine optimization, email marketing, and video marketing in expanding brand reach and engagement. By harnessing these digital tools, businesses can connect with a wider audience and drive brand awareness and customer acquisition.

However, building a successful brand is an ongoing process. Continuous improvement, proactive communication, and a commitment to delivering exceptional customer service are crucial in nurturing customer relationships and building trust. Businesses must also keep a pulse on industry trends, monitor competitors, and adapt their strategies accordingly.

Ultimately, success in the bathroom fittings industry requires a combination of strategic branding, customer-centricity, and effective marketing. This book serves as a roadmap for aspiring leaders in the industry, providing valuable insights, practical strategies, and real-world examples to guide them towards brand success.

As the bathroom fittings industry continues to evolve and new challenges and opportunities arise, it is crucial for businesses to stay agile and adapt their branding strategies. By staying true to their brand values, consistently delivering exceptional experiences, and embracing innovation, businesses can establish themselves as leaders and carve a niche in the market.

"The Branding Blueprint: Become A Leader in Bathroom Fittings Industry" is not only a guide but a source of inspiration and motivation for entrepreneurs, business owners, and marketing professionals. It is a testament to the power of branding in driving business success and creating a lasting impact in the bathroom fittings industry.

As readers embark on their branding journey, may this book serve as a trusted companion, offering guidance, insights, and practical advice to help them navigate the challenges and unlock the immense potential that lies within their brands. Remember, building a successful brand is a continuous process, and with dedication, innovation, and a customer-centric approach, you have the power to become a leader in the bathroom fittings industry.

Take the first step towards becoming a leader in the bathroom fittings industry. Start implementing the strategies and insights shared in this book today! Unlock the power of branding, differentiate your brand, and build lasting customer relationships.

Let **"The Branding Blueprint: Become A Leader In Bathroom Fittings Industry"** be your guide to success.

Through personalized consultations, workshops, and implementation support, Amit Jain can be your trusted partner in transforming your business and positioning yourself as a leader in the bathroom fittings industry. Take advantage of his expertise and let him guide you towards achieving your goals.

Contact Amit Jain today and embark on a transformative journey towards brand excellence.

Don't wait, take action and shape the future of your business!!!

With Best Wishes,
Amit Jain
amit@amit-jain.in